**At Issue**

# What Is the Future of Higher Education?

# Other Books in the At Issue Series:

# At Issue

# What Is the Future of Higher Education?

*Roman Espejo, Book Editor*

**GREENHAVEN PRESS**
*A part of Gale, Cengage Learning*

GALE
CENGAGE Learning·

Farmington Hills, Mich • San Francisco • New York • Waterville, Maine
Meriden, Conn • Mason, Ohio • Chicago

GALE
CENGAGE Learning·

Patricia Coryell, *Vice President & Publisher, New Products & GVRL*
Douglas Dentino, *Manager, New Products*
Judy Galens, *Acquisitions Editor*

**LIBRARY OF CONGRESS CATALOGING-IN-PUBLICATION DATA**

What is the future of higher education? / Roman Espejo, book editor.
    pages cm. -- (At issue)
Includes bibliographical references and index.
ISBN 978-0-7377-7201-2 (hardcover) — ISBN 978-0-7377-7202-9 (pbk.)
    1. Education, Higher—Aims and objectives. 2. Universities and colleges—United States. I. Espejo, Roman, 1977–
    LA227.4.W466 2015
    378.00973—dc23
                                                              2014040160

Printed in Mexico
1 2 3 4 5 6 7 19 18 17 16 15

# Contents

# Introduction

From the University of Phoenix's sprawling network of 112 campuses to Drexel University's distance learning classes to Le Cordon Bleu's focus on the culinary arts, for-profit educational institutions vary in size, scope, and specialty. What is controversial about them, of course, is that they are profitable. "For-profit colleges are run by companies that operate under the demands of investors and stockholders. These institutions are privately run and exist, at least in part, to earn money for their owners,"[1] states the National Association for College Admission Counseling. In 2012, revenues for for-profit college and universities reached $27 billion, in comparison to $317 billion at public nonprofit institutions and $162 billion at private nonprofit institutions.

In the United States, the sector has experienced a boom since the 1990s. "They once fulfilled an important role in the country's education system. Traditionally, they were small and tended to offer vocational qualifications or part-time programs to cater to working adults.

"But over the past three decades, for-profit higher education has grown quickly,"[2] observes the *Economist*. "In 1980, just 1 percent of American students were enrolled at a for-profit college; by 2008, 8 percent were. Among black and Hispanic students, who are under-represented at traditional universities, the proportion is far higher."

With this boom, for-profit colleges and universities are the subject of growing scrutiny. One criticism is that tuitions at these institutions are much higher than at nonprofit state col-

1. National Association for College Admission Counseling, "The Low-Down on For-Profit Colleges," www.nacacnet.org (accessed August 8, 2014). www.nacacnet.org /issues-action/LegislativeNews/Pages/For-Profit-Colleges.aspx.
2. *Economist*, "Why Do Americans Mistrust For-Profit Universities?" July 2, 2013. www.economist.com/blogs/economist-explains/2013/07/economist-explains-0#st hash.IW3JN1Jj.dpuf.

leges, but much less is spent in the classroom. "Indeed, they typically spend a lot more on marketing their courses than they do on teaching them. This may explain why the majority of students on their degree programmes drop out long before they graduate,"[3] maintains the *Economist*, explaining that in the 2008 to 2009 school year the average student studied at a for-profit institution for only four months.

Additionally, many critics accuse these schools of exploiting students and federal student aid—Pell Grants and subsidized student loans—with their eyes on the bottom line, not education. "Phoenix alone is on pace to reap $1-billion from Pell Grants this year, along with $4-billion from federal loans. A quarter of all federal aid goes to for-profits, while they enroll only 10 percent of students,"[4] purports Kevin Carey, director of the education policy program at the New America Foundation. Under pressure from for-profit universities, he adds, people enrolled in these schools go into deep debt without moving forward in their professional lives. "Unfortunately, a large and growing number of graduates of for-profit colleges are having trouble paying those loans back," Carey asserts. "Horror stories of aggressive recruiters inducing students to take out huge loans for nearly worthless degrees are filling the news."[5]

One such formerly hopeful and currently debt-saddled graduate of a for-profit college is Margie Donaldson of Detroit, Michigan, who told her story to *Mother Jones* magazine. After leaving her $80,000 a year job at Chrysler through a buyout, Donaldson enrolled at ITT Technical Institute to complete her unfinished bachelor's in criminal justice, taking on $75,000 in debt. She was unable to find full-time work after graduating five years later; the degree Donaldson earned is

3. Ibid.
4. Kevin Carey, "Why Do You Think They're Called For-Profit Colleges?" *Chronicle of Higher Education*, July 25, 2010. http://chronicle.com/article/Why-Do-You-Think -Theyre/123660/.
5. Ibid.

not regionally credited—therefore immaterial to employers—and her credits cannot be transferred to another college or university. With three children to support on $1,400 a month as a part-time anger management counselor, Donaldson regrets her decision to not attend a much less expensive community college instead. "It's almost like I'm like a paycheck away from going back to where I grew up,"[6] she says.

Despite the horror stories, for-profit colleges and universities are not demonized by everyone. William G. Tierney, codirector of the University of Southern California's Pullias Center for Higher Education, sees a productive future for them. For instance, Tierney believes that only credible institutions will survive. "Any booming industry brings in not only reputable business people but also con men (and women) who could care less about quality,"[7] he contends. "If the industry is to grow, however, the con men have to go away." Tierney also predicts that legislation, as seen in California, will allow noninstitutional entities such as for-profits to offer common undergraduate courses in innovative ways. "If you and I are able to develop a quality English 101 course with clear learning objectives that could be measured, then why would we need to develop a for-profit or non-profit institution? Why could we not simply do this as a start-up company with multiple business nodes?,"[8] he speculates. Finally, Tierney suggests that these schools will diversify into "boutique institutions" providing niche curricula and training for the students who seek them. "Think of the beer industry. There remains a market for Budweiser and Miller, but micro-brewing is also thriving.

6. Quoted in Yasmeen Qureshi, Sarah Gross, and Lisa Desai, "Screw U: How For-Profit Colleges Rip You Off," *Mother Jones*, January 31, 2014. www.motherjones.com/politics/2014/01/for-profit-college-student-debt.

7. William G. Tierney, "Three Future Trends in For-Profit Higher Education," The EvoLLLution, July 8, 2013. www.evolllution.com/opinions/future-trends-for-profit-higher-education.

8. Ibid.

Some consumers prefer a particular taste to the more main-stream brews. The same will be true in higher education,"[9] he persists.

Others come to the defense of the sector's reportedly low graduation rates. Henry Bienen, vice chairman of the board of for-profit Rasmussen College and professor emeritus at Northwestern University, reasons that the case is not the same at every school. "As for career placement, more than 90% of graduates of Rasmussen College, with which I am associated, are currently employed, despite the recession. Across for-profits, placement rates for students who get degrees in medical technology, business administration, information technology and design are all high,"[10] he insists. Moreover, Bienen offers an alternative perspective to explain why dropping out is a higher risk among these students. "Education officials and critics should realize that increased access is likely to mean strains on graduation rates. But that is not an argument against offering nontraditional students an education that would otherwise be beyond reach,"[11] he argues.

The growth of for-profit colleges and universities can be attributed to faster Internet speeds, better hardware and software, and the further improvement of online classes. But technology itself is only one driver of change at postsecondary institutions; for instance, mounting tuition is now a national crisis, prompting a reexamination of the value of a four-year degree and exploration of novel approaches to learning. *At Issue: What Is the Future of Higher Education?* investigates these topics and more.

9. Ibid.
10. Henry Bienen, "In Defense of For-Profit Colleges," *Wall Street Journal*, July 24, 2010. www.wsj.com/news/articles/SB10001424052748703724104575378933954267308.
11. Ibid.

1

# Experts Have Diverse Predictions for the Future of Higher Education

*Janna Anderson, Jan Lauren Boyles, and Lee Rainie*

*Janna Anderson is a full professor and director of the Imagining the Internet Center at Elon University and a researcher at Pew Research Center's Internet & American Life Project. Jan Lauren Boyles is an adjunct professor of journalism and doctoral fellow at American University and a Google Journalism Fellow at the Pew Research Center's Journalism Project. Lee Rainie is director of the Internet & American Life Project at Pew Research Center.*

*From cloud-based computing to digital textbooks to "just-in-time" information gathering, the technological disruptions of the Internet have led to a reexamination of modern universities and colleges. In a 2012 survey, experts and stakeholders offered their predictions for higher education in 2020; 39 percent agreed that it will remain largely the same as today, while 69 percent agreed that it will experience significant technology-centered changes. The themes and arguments addressed the adoption of new teaching approaches; the economic realities driving technological innovations; the divisive issue of distance learning; the role of brick-and-mortar schools; the maintenance of traditional methods; the emergence of collaborative education and peer-to-peer learning; and trends in credentialing, certification, and degree customization.*

For a millennium, universities have been considered the main societal hub for knowledge and learning. And for a millennium, the basic structures of how universities produce and disseminate knowledge and evaluate students have survived intact through the sweeping societal changes created by technology—the moveable-type printing press, the Industrial Revolution, the telegraph, telephone, radio, television, and computers.

Today, though, the business of higher education seems to some as susceptible to tech disruption as other information-centric industries such as the news media, magazines and journals, encyclopedias, music, motion pictures, and television. The transmission of knowledge need no longer be tethered to a college campus. The technical affordances of cloud-based computing, digital textbooks, mobile connectivity, high-quality streaming video, and "just-in-time" information gathering have pushed vast amounts of knowledge to the "placeless" Web. This has sparked a robust re-examination of the modern university's mission and its role within networked society.

One major driver of the debate about the future of the university centers on its beleaguered business model. Students and parents, stretched by rising tuition costs, are increasingly challenging the affordability of a college degree as well as the diploma's ultimate value as an employment credential.

---

*Higher education administrators—sometimes constrained by budgetary shortfalls and change-resistant academic cultures—are trying to respond and retool.*

---

A March 2012 study by the Pew Research Center for the People & the Press found that 60% of American adults viewed universities as having a positive effect on how things are going in the country and 84% of college graduates say that the expense of going to college was a good investment for them. Yet another Pew Research Center survey in 2011 found that 75% of adults say college is too expensive for most Americans to afford. Moreover, 57% said that the higher education system in the U.S. fails to provide students with good value for the money they and their families spend.

This set of circumstances has catalyzed the marketplace. Universities are watching competitors encroach on their traditional mission. The challengers include for-profit universities, nonprofit learning organizations such as the Khan Academy, commercial providers of lecture series, online services such as iTunes U, and a host of specialized training centers that provide instruction and credentials for particular trades and professions. All these can easily scale online instruction delivery more quickly than can brick-and-mortar institutions.

Consequently, higher education administrators—sometimes constrained by budgetary shortfalls and change-resistant academic cultures—are trying to respond and retool. The Pew Research Center 2011 study found in a survey of college presidents that more than three-fourths (77%) of respondents said their institution offered online course offerings. Half said they believe that most students at their schools will be enrolled in at least some online classes within the next 10 years.

The debate about the urgency for change and the pace of change on campus was highlighted in recent weeks at the University of Virginia. The school's governing body, the Board of Visitors, voted to oust school President Teresa Sullivan, arguing that she was not pursuing change quickly enough. After a faculty, student, and alumni uproar, the Board reversed course and reinstated her. Still, the school announced within a week of her return that it was joining Coursera—a privately held, online instructional delivery firm. That meant it would join numerous other elite research institutions, including Duke University, Johns Hopkins University, Princeton University, Stanford University, the University of Pennsylvania, and others as part of Coursera's online consortium. As of mid-2012,

Coursera's massively open online courses (MOOCs) were provided free to its students—enabling unfettered, global access for millions to engage with some of the country's most prestigious universities. Other start-ups such as MITx, 2tor, and Udacity are attracting similarly staggering, six-figure student enrollments.

Experimentation and innovation are proliferating. Some colleges are delving into hybrid learning environments, which employ online and offline instruction and interaction with professors. Others are channeling efforts into advanced teleconferencing and distance learning platforms—with streaming video and asynchronous discussion boards—to heighten engagement online.

Even as all this change occurs, there are those who argue that the core concept and method of universities will not radically change. They argue that mostly unfulfilled predictions of significant improvement in the effectiveness and wider distribution of education accompany every major new communication technology. In the early days of their evolution, radio, television, personal computers—and even the telephone—were all predicted to be likely to revolutionize formal education. Nevertheless, the standardized knowledge-transmission model is primarily the same today as it was when students started gathering at the University of Bologna in 1088.

## Where We Might Be in 2020

Imagine where we might be in 2020. The Pew Research Center's Internet & American Life Project and Elon University's Imagining the Internet Center asked digital stakeholders to weigh two scenarios for 2020. One posited substantial change and the other projected only modest change in higher education. Some 1,021 experts and stakeholders responded.

39% agreed with a scenario that articulated modest change by the end of the decade:

*In 2020, higher education will not be much different from the way it is today. While people will be accessing more resources in classrooms through the use of large screens, teleconferencing, and personal wireless smart devices, most universities will mostly require in-person, on-campus attendance of students most of the time at courses featuring a lot of traditional lectures. Most universities' assessment of learning and their requirements for graduation will be about the same as they are now.*

60% agreed with a scenario outlining more change:

*By 2020, higher education will be quite different from the way it is today. There will be mass adoption of teleconferencing and distance learning to leverage expert resources. Significant numbers of learning activities will move to individualized, just-in-time learning approaches. There will be a transition to "hybrid" classes that combine online learning components with less-frequent on-campus, in-person class meetings. Most universities' assessment of learning will take into account more individually-oriented outcomes and capacities that are relevant to subject mastery. Requirements for graduation will be significantly shifted to customized outcomes.*

---

*The universities that survive will do so mainly by becoming highly adaptive.*

---

Respondents were asked to select the one statement of the two scenarios above with which they mostly agreed; the question was framed this way in order to encourage survey participants to share spirited and deeply considered written elaborations about the potential future of higher education. While 60% agreed with the statement that education will be transformed between now and the end of the decade, a significant number of the survey participants said the true outcome will encompass portions of both scenarios. Just 1% of survey takers did not respond.

Here are some of the major themes and arguments they made:

## New Teaching Approaches

*Higher education will vigorously adopt new teaching approaches, propelled by opportunity and efficiency as well as student and parent demands.*

- Several respondents echoed the core argument offered by Alex Halavais, associate professor at Quinnipiac University and vice president of the Association of Internet Researchers, who wrote: "There will be far more extreme changes institutionally in the next few years, and the universities that survive will do so mainly by becoming highly adaptive . . . The most interesting shifts in post-secondary education may happen outside of universities, or at least on the periphery of traditional universities. There may be universities that remain focused on the traditional lecture and test, but there will be less demand for them."

- Charlie Firestone, executive director of the Communications and Society program at the Aspen Institute, wrote: "The timeline might be a bit rushed, but education—higher and K-12—*has* to change with the technology. The technology will allow for more individualized, passion-based learning by the student, greater access to master teaching, and more opportunities for students to connect to others— mentors, peers, sources—for enhanced learning experiences."

- Mike Liebhold, senior researcher and distinguished fellow at The Institute for the Future, predicted that market forces will advance emergent content delivery methods: "Under current and foreseeable economic conditions, traditional classroom instruction will become decreasingly viable financially. As high-speed networks become more widely accessible tele-education and hybrid instruction will become more widely employed."

- Jeff Jarvis, director of the Tow-Knight Center for Entrepreneurial Journalism at the City University of New York Graduate School of Journalism, placed the debate in broader historical context: "Will there still be universities? Likely, but not certain . . . [there is] the idea that our current educational system, start to end, is built for an industrial era, churning out students like widgets who are taught to churn out widgets themselves. That is a world where there is one right answer: We spew it from a lectern; we expect it to be spewed back in a test. That kind of education does not produce the innovators who would invent Google. The real need for education in the economy will be re-education. As industries go through disruption and jobs are lost forever, people will need to be retrained for new roles. Our present educational structure is not built for that, but in that I see great entrepreneurial opportunity."

- P.F. Anderson, emerging technologies librarian at the University of Michigan-Ann Arbor, predicted seismic shifts within the academy, writing, "The very concept of what a university is, what academia is, what adult learning is, all of these are changing profoundly. If you think back to the original pur-poses of universities, what they have been doing recently has pivoted roughly 180 degrees."

# Economic Realities and Technological Innovation

*Economic realities will drive technological innovation forward by 2020, creating less uniformity in higher education.*

- Donald G. Barnes, visiting professor at Guangxi University in China and former director of the Science Advisory Board at the U.S. Environmental Protection Agency, predicted, "The high and growing cost of university education cannot be sustained, particularly in the light of the growing global demand for such education. Therefore, there is already a rush to utilize the new medium of the Internet as a means of delivering higher education experience and products in more economical and efficient modes."

- Tapio Varis, professor emeritus at the University of Tampere and principal research associate with the UN [United Nations] Educational, Scientific, and Cultural Organization, maintained that heightened inequalities may arise based upon instructional delivery formats. "The economic reasons will determine much of the destiny of higher education," he wrote. "Traditional face-to-face higher education will become a privilege of a few, and there will be demand for global standardization of some fields of education which also will lower the level in many cases."

- Sean Mead, director of solutions architecture, valuation, and analytics for Mead, Mead & Clark, Interbrand, noted that institutions will stratify based upon their respective concentrations of teaching, research, or service. "Forced into greater accountability at the same time as Baby Boomer retirements revitalize the faculties, universities will undergo widespread reformation," he said. "Some will refocus professorial metrics from running up publication counts to the profession of teaching and delivering strong educations. Others will engage the community in outreach efforts to make learning more accessible. More universities will follow the MIT [Massachusetts Institute of Technology] and Stanford examples of serving the public with free access to course materials and courses . . . There will be increasing corporate involvement in universities, including better communication of the knowledge that is developed and housed there. Research will increasingly be driven out from behind the high-premium-pay walls of academic journals and into the open, where scholars and the public can more easily benefit from federally funded and grant-supported research projects."

---

*Some institutions will focus on facilitating virtual environments and may lose any physical aspect.*

---

## Distance Learning

*"Distance learning" is a divisive issue. It is viewed with disdain by many who don't see it as effective; others anticipate great advances in knowledge-sharing tools by 2020.*

- Online course offerings generally fail to mirror the robust face-to-face interaction that occurs within the physical classroom, warned Sam Punnett, president of FAD Research Inc. "On-screen learning is appropriate in some instances, particularly as a supplement to the classroom," he said, "but it will always be inferior in the quality of information exchange and interaction. In 2020 it is my hope that programs that employ instructors who are 'in the room' will be generally acknowledged to be in a separate tier."

- On the other hand, Peter Pinch, director of technology for WGBH, a public media company, predicted renewed innovation in remote learning platforms will mark the university by 2020. "As communications technologies improve and we learn how to use them better, the requirement for people to meet face-to-face for effective teaching and learning will diminish," he predicted. "Some institutions will focus on facilitating virtual environments and may lose any physical aspect. Other institutions will focus on the most high-value face-to-face interactions, such as group discussions and labs, and will shed commodity teaching activities like large lectures."

• Fred Hapgood, technology author and consultant, and writer for *Wired, Discover,* and other tech and science publications, said, "*The* key challenge of the next five years—I say '*the*' because of the importance of education for the entire global labor force and the importance of reducing its crushing costs—will be developing ways of integrating distance learning with social networking. I am confident this challenge will be met."

## Bricks Replaced by Clicks?

'Bricks' replaced by 'clicks'? Some say universities' influence could be altered as new technology options emerge; others say 'locatedness' is still vital for an optimal outcome.

• An anonymous survey respondent noted, "The age of brick-and-mortar dinosaur schools is about to burst—another bubble ready to pop. The price is too high; it's grossly inflated and the return on investment isn't there. Online learning will be in the ascendant. There will be more international interactions; I believe we will see somewhat of a return to a Socratic model of single sage to self-selecting student group, but instead of the Acropolis, the site will be the Internet, and the students will be from everywhere."

- Another anonymous survey participant wrote, "Several forces will impact this: the general overall increase in the levels of education globally, the developing world using Web and cell technology to jump over intermediate technologies, the high cost of face-to-face instruction, the improvement of AI [artificial intelligence] as a factor in individualizing education, the passing of the Baby Boomers as educators in the system, the demand for Millennials and beyond for relevant learning models, China will develop a leading learning format, first to educate its population and then expand it to teach the world."

- Matthew Allen, professor of Internet Studies at Curtin University in Perth, Australia, and past president of the Association of Internet Researchers, visualizes 2020's ivory tower through a socio-cultural lens: "While education is being, and has been already, profoundly influenced by technologies, nevertheless it is a deeply social and political institution in our cultures. Universities are not just portals where students access learning, they are places in which people develop as social beings, in some quite specifically institutional ways. Therefore technology will change the way learning occurs and the way it is assessed, and it definitely means there is more blending of learning activities on- and offline, but it will not—for the majority—change the fundamental locatedness of university education."

- There were also people who said technology should never drive change. An anonymous respondent wrote, "Technology is no substitute for traditional education. 'Vir bonus dicendi peritus' or the good man who can speak well will not be brought about by techno-based thinking." . . .

---

*We've got to move to much more individual, hyperlinked learning experiences.*

---

## Retaining Traditional Methods

*Universities will adopt new pedagogical approaches while retaining the core of traditional methods.*

- Richard D. Titus, a seed-funding venture capitalist at his own fund, Octavian Ventures, predicted, "The future is a hybrid of both of the approaches. No one can disagree that higher education needs—no, requires—a complete rethink. Our current toolsets and thinking are over 400 years old and give little regard to the changes in society, resources, or access, which facilitate both greater specialization and broader access than at any time in the previous two centuries."

- Face-to-face instruction, complemented by online interaction, makes up a hybrid model that many survey participants foresee. Melinda Blau, a freelance journalist and author, wrote, "The future will hold *both* outcomes. It depends on the course of study and the college."

- Susan Crawford, a professor at Harvard University's Kennedy School of Government who previously served as President [Barack] Obama's Special Assistant for Science, Technology, and Innovation Policy, wrote that she expects an influx of customized course content will be fused with the traditional elements of a multidisciplinary college education. "We've got to move to much more individual, hyperlinked learning experiences," she said. "At the same time, modeling good behavior and good thinking style remains something useful that teachers do for students . . . I'm hopeful that we'll find a way of educating that inculcates the values a true liberal arts education was supposed to support—lifelong learning, lifelong foolishness (hymn to Stuart Brand), and lifelong awe."

- An anonymous participant wrote, "I expect a huge movement towards knowledge-management tools that enhance the learning practice and focus on each individual path while maintaining engagement at a social level. This could make the learning experience tailored to each individual and at the same time aggregate responses and perceptions from a large group of students in order to direct toward specific learning goals."

- Another anonymous respondent predicted, "Universities will continue their transition to hybrid classes using online learning components and occasional in-person meetings, while smaller colleges will both adopt online capabilities and technologies to promote access to remote resources while maintaining a focus on in-person, on-campus attendance of seminars and (some) lectures. The length of the learning period (the traditional four-year degree) may change as a result of the focus on combined learning, with integration of more off-site activities with the traditional scholastic setting. I also think that economic factors over the next few years may promote the evolution of educational institutions along the lines of a transition to hybrid learning, while also preventing any mass adoption of just-in-time approaches."

## Collaborative Education

*Collaborative education with peer-to-peer learning will become a bigger reality and will challenge the lecture format and focus on "learning how to learn."*

- Autonomy will be shifted away from the sole lecturer in tomorrow's university classrooms, maintains Bob Frankston, a computing pioneer and the co-developer and marketer of VisiCalc. "Ideally, people will learn to educate themselves with teachers acting as mentors and guides," he wrote.

- By 2020, universities should re-examine how technology can enhance students' critical thinking and information acquisition skills, noted Wesley George, principal engineer for the Advanced Technology Group at Time Warner Cable. "The educational system is largely broken," he said. "It's too focused on the result of getting a degree rather than teaching people *how* to learn: how to digest huge amounts of information, craft a cogent argument in favor of or against a topic, and how to think for oneself. Individuals learn differently, and we are starting to finally have the technology to embrace that instead of catering to the lowest common denominator."

- Hal Varian, chief economist at Google, said, "Just-in-Time learning is a very important phenomenon that will have a big role to play in the future . . . Universities should, and I hope will, focus more on 'how to learn' rather than simply 'learning.'"

- Universities should additionally ensure their graduates are poised for 2020's job market, maintains danah boyd, a senior researcher at Microsoft Research. "Higher education will not change very fast, although it should," she wrote. "But what's at stake has nothing to do with the amount of technology being used. What's at stake has to do with the fact that universities are not structured to provide the skills that are needed for a rapidly changing labor, creative force."

## Credentialing, Certification, and Degree Customization

*Competency credentialing and certification are likely . . .*

- Rick Holmgren, chief information officer at Allegheny College, said, "Many institutions, particularly large state institutions, will have shifted to competency-driven credentialing, which may not require traditional class work at all, but rather the demonstration of competency."

- Morley Winograd, co-author of *Millennial Momentum: How a New Generation is Remaking America,* similarly argued, "The deflection point for the more fundamental change will occur when universities no longer grant degrees, but rather certify knowledge and skill levels, in much more finite ways as your scenario envisions. Major university brands will offer such certificates based on their standards for certifying various competencies that employers will be identifying for their new hires."

*. . . Yet institutional barriers may prevent widespread degree customization.*

- Scalability may present a hurdle toward achieving personalization, argued David Ellis, director of communication studies at York University in Toronto. "Customizing education is too complicated for large institutions," he argued. "And if outcomes are made too personal, a perception of bias or unfairness is likely to arise."

- Joan Lorden, provost and vice chancellor for academic affairs at University of North Carolina-Charlotte, predicted, "Customized assessment is unlikely. There is still a general sense in most university faculties that there are certain foundational elements that must be addressed in a high-quality educational experience."

2

# The Online Challenge to Higher Education

*William B. Bonvillian and Susan R. Singer*

*William B. Bonvillian is director of the Massachusetts Institute of Technology's Washington office, on the adjunct faculty at Georgetown and Johns Hopkins School of Advanced International Studies (SAIS), and a former member of the National Research Council's Board on Science Education (BOSE). Susan R. Singer is a Laurence McKinley Gould Professor of Biology at Carleton College and has also served on BOSE.*

*Advances in broadband Internet, mobile technology, and the science of learning will fundamentally transform the lecture model of higher education. Hailed as "new magic" in education reform, massive online open courses (MOOCs) present an opportunity to revolutionize the availability and presentation of classes—particularly in science, technology, engineering, and math (STEM)— bringing dynamic visualization of and interaction with data and new ways to map content and core ideas to students worldwide. While other teaching components, academic evaluation, and laboratories will continue to require face-to-face communication, MOOCs will evolve as a disruptive force; the functions of academic research institutions will not be replaced, but the colleges and universities that survive will blend MOOCs with conventional education.*

National Academy of Engineering Presational Academy of Engineering President Charles Vest tells a story about the roles of people and computers. In 1997, IBM's Deep Blue computer beat chess master Garry Kasparov; since then, chess masters have also periodically beaten computers. But Vest notes that the combined team of a computer and chess master always beats either the computer or the chess master alone. This says much about the future of higher education, especially in the sciences.

The idea has been growing that universities will change dramatically, and perhaps largely fade away, under the spread of online education increasingly enabled by improvements in broadband Internet access and new mobile devices. Recent years have also seen advances in the science of learning that are enabling society and researchers to look at new education approaches. The accumulating evidence challenges the model that has long dominated higher education: the sage on the stage; that is, the lecture.

These two potential revolutions—online education and in the science of learning—are on parallel but unconnected tracks heading toward a fundamentally different system of higher education. They need to be linked to optimize both.

A key component of the emerging educational world is massive online open courses, popularly called MOOCs, a term just a few years old. Early MOOC providers were for-profit firms that saw opportunities to capture higher education markets. At the University of Phoenix, a leader in online education, total enrollment by 2012 was approximately 308,000. At Kaplan University, another major online provider, enrollment was 78,000. Universities have responded to this market threat. At Coursera, an initial university MOOC platform originating from science faculty at Stanford, 62 universities now offer at least one course, including 16 recently added from abroad. Coursera adopted a for-profit model and obtained venture funding. Udacity, another for-profit MOOC provider developed by Stanford faculty, recently announced a master's degree in computer science program, in conjunction with the Georgia Institute of Technology and AT&T.

*Developing quality online courses, assuming they are not mere videos of lectures, is much more expensive than developing a physical classroom course.*

Concerned about the implications of grafting a for-profit approach onto nonprofit institutions, the Massachusetts Institute of Technology (MIT), later joined by Harvard University, launched edX as a nonprofit educational venture, with $60 million in experimental funding from the two schools. The edX alliance now has 27 university members, including 6 leading universities in Asia. Each school is creating courses for its own use and the use of others. The plan has been to post the courses and make them available without charge, although charges are contemplated in the future for students seeking a certificate of course completion.

The first edX course, from MIT, was on computer and electronic circuit design, directly taken from MIT's introductory circuit design course. It initially drew some 154,000 participants worldwide. Other MOOC providers saw comparable initial numbers. No one had seen such numbers attending a single course. Most of these early viewers proved to be "shoppers," testing the buzz and content. Some 7,000 people eventually completed the edX course for a certificate. Even this number is breathtaking—60% more than MIT's undergraduate enrollment. edX, operating since 2012, recently counted its millionth student.

Online students proved to be self-assembling, assisting each other and organizing online and in-person discussion groups. edX has become the theater, staging the show with the participating universities developing the course content around evolving edX design standards. edX is developing and offering the platform and assessment software, serving as the common technical support mechanism. Developing quality online courses, assuming they are not mere videos of lectures, is much more expensive than developing a physical classroom course. Although the courses so far are free and universally available online, schools offering MOOCs will need to charge for completion certificates to cover development. However, the MOOC business model is by no means clear. Schools are starting to see that alongside their established university, they may have to form a "Pixar" branch.

## MOOCs and Educational Reform

Many politicians in the United States seem to feel that MOOCs represent a kind of "new magic": online higher education for free. Although never explicitly stated this way, conservative politicians seem to be hoping that for-profit online higher education can finally rid the republic of those pesky, left-wing universities. Progressive politicians, on the other hand, seem to be hoping MOOCs will end what they view as outrageous university tuition rates, driving tuition through the floor and making higher education more accessible than ever before.

This desire for lower costs can be seen in Florida, where the governor issued a challenge, and 23 state colleges agreed to offer the option of a $10,000 bachelor's degree. California, which has been systematically slashing state support for higher education, recently passed legislation requiring state universities to give credit for online courses where there are not enough physical classroom seats for students. The pressure to cede education to online courses is growing as states cut funding for higher education to pay for the growth of Medicaid expenditures and prisons. Because some 72% of U.S. higher education is provided by state-funded higher education systems, this is powerful pressure.

Given these pressures, what will happen to the campus—to residential higher education? Although MOOCs will affect all types of higher education, from community colleges to private colleges to the several tiers of regional state universities to for-profit education providers, we focus here on the first tier of research universities, public and private, and particularly on education in science, technology, engineering, and mathematics (the STEM fields).

The research university has evolved over the past 150 years or so into the most important home for scientific advancement; it is the base system for global knowledge. The research university is a comparatively new creation in the United States, modeled in the late 19th century on the German university and coming into its own through the massive federal investments in R&D during World War II and the subsequent Cold War. The brilliance of this model was in combining research and education, so learning became hands-on, with research and learning being mutually reinforcing and learning continuous. This learning-by-doing model, although remarkably effective, has also contributed to the high cost of undergraduate science education, as students need increasingly expensive labs.

The entry of the lab into science education was a creation of mid-19th century reformers such as William Barton Rogers, who helped shift natural science away from the lecture model and its accompanying recitation and memorization. This critical education reform was followed by the introduction of the seminar in the first part of the 20th century. Education philanthropist Edward Harkness, a Standard Oil heir who felt that middle-range students (such as himself) were left out of a system that focused only on students at the top and bottom of classes, funded Phillips Exeter Academy faculty to study Oxford University and Cambridge University models for education ideas. Finding that the remarkable one-on-one tutorial system at those schools was prohibitively expensive, the Phillips Exeter faculty created the seminar of 12 or so students around an oval "Harkness table" in the 1930s to bring all participating students into the common discourse. The model spread to the Ivy League and widely to U.S. universities for upper-level courses.

If society can get the model right, there is an opportunity for worldwide availability of courses. MOOCs are potentially an even more transformative revolution. They may be a particularly interesting new tool for STEM education. This is because problem-solving in these fields may fit more readily into online courses than does the discourse emphasis in humanities or social science courses. Online learning can enable dynamic visualization of data and the ability to interact with that data, allowing the ability to identify new data patterns and influencing factors. It opens new ways for mapping the content and core ideas of a field, with new possibilities for the representation of both information and knowledge. And it can be great tool for realtime assessment of content acquisition and knowledge transfer and application, with the ability to improve reinforcement of content.

---

*At least in the near term, the most effective education will combine online and face-to-face approaches into "blended learning" that captures the best of both worlds.*

---

Even as online education advances, vital education components will remain face-to-face at least for some time to come. Developing expertise through oral expression and presentations will remain especially critical. Online education simply cannot handle these aspects of learning very well so far. Conventional education methods can also effectively promote written analysis. Machine evaluation of written papers is improving, and edX, for example, has a team working on this technology. But although software can capture key words and rubrics supplied by faculty (what might be called established concepts), it will not be good at recognizing out-of-the-box new ideas or evaluating ideas with fresh approaches. For a very long time to come, writing will require human assessment, except for more straightforward assignments.

Conventional education will also remain vital in research, where online capabilities can be limiting. Performing research is central to learning by doing in science; indeed, it is what scientists do. Although computer simulations and modeling can capture elements of how to perform research, in many fields the student ultimately needs to be at a lab bench or in the field, interacting with a research team for project-based learning. Online features can enhance research. For example, data visualization and display and computer simulations can be critical tools, and MIT has an "iLab" for high-school science students, where they can run real experiments online from any location on real MIT equipment. But there is no getting around the reality that research in many fields requires critical face-to-face dynamics and interactions with the natural world that will be hard to replace.

## Blending for Success

In the end, then, MOOCs may change everything, but they will not necessarily kill everything. Indeed, at least in the near term, the most effective education will combine online and face-to-face approaches into "blended learning" that captures the best of both worlds.

In this scenario, online education will continue to evolve. In some ways, it will become better at doing some of the jobs that are the hallmarks of conventional education. For example, with growing broadband capability, it will be possible to further build online discussion groups, and the videos will increasingly be able to use high-definition capability for improved realism. Machine writing evaluation will get better. Even now, for shorter papers, in which software can increasingly evaluate key word use, rubrics, and core concepts, MIT's machine grading software matches the score of a human grader as accurately as a second human grader 85% of the time. And as noted, research can be complemented by online simulation and modeling and can offer online access to lab equipment and the ability to run experiments online.

There is a larger point, as well. "Face-to-face" conventionally has implied physical proximity, but there are significant learning areas where, as technology continues to improve, face-to-face is transforming into "person-to-person," where virtual personal connections are online. Personalized education is not likely to remain the sole province of face-to-face education.

So even as online and face-to-face approaches manage a certain détente, online is likely to become an ever more disruptive force. It is now well accepted that new firms embracing new technologies can disrupt and eventually displace legacy firms.

Clayton Christensen, the business professor who developed this field, argues that when nonprofit higher education was a service-only sector, it was protected. Its service model had long since absorbed book technology as its one technology base, already a mature sector after five centuries of development. It had been successful in evading any significant new technology component, facing only modest incursions from the private-sector online education system, which had been slowly evolving. When a point was reached where online entry could scale, with significant broadband access and smartphone entry, the way was open for a new technology component to enter higher education. It was the arrival of this new technology that created the possibility of disruptive displacement for the existing higher education system.

Christensen proposes an analogy: Online is the steamship. Early steam engines were very inefficient, requiring great volumes of wood or coal. They could not power a ship across an ocean, but they found a niche market, starting out on rivers. Steam engines, although initially inefficient, had a compelling advantage; they could move steadily upriver into current and wind, stopping when necessary to refuel. As the engines became more reliable and efficient, they became suitable for longer trips. Shipmakers then developed a hybrid technology that incorporated steam engines into sailing ships. Sidewheels were replaced by more efficient screw propellers, and the development of steel hulls made it possible to build larger ships that could carry more fuel. Sails were eventually eliminated, and the hybrid technology was replaced by steam-only vessels. Will this be the higher education story? Will blended learning (the hybrid model) eventually fade and be displaced by an online steamship? Will universities go the way of sailing ships?

Even as it proves disruptive, however, online education will continue to depend on conventional education, especially universities, for some time to come. The fundamental reason is that if universities were to disappear, the institutional source for course content would collapse over time. Universities are also research engines as well as teaching and learning centers; at least in science, that research side has a separate funding system that could be maintained, apart from education tuition (although tuition revenues provide research subsidies, because universities do not fully recover their indirect costs from the federal government). In a knowledge economy, there is no substitute for universities, which are literally innovation systems that are critical for societal growth. With industry research ever more focused on incremental advances in later development stages, the breakthrough stage increasingly is a university role, using federal science research funds. University research, by proving a foundation for learning by doing, is also central to science education.

Although there is no real replacement for many research university functions, it is possible that the university in its present form will survive only if it significantly reforms its face-to-face learning model. Its age-old primary delivery tool, the lecture, is no longer the optimal model. A head-to-head competition between a live talking head in a classroom and an online presentation with assessment and interactive features built in is not a winning proposition in the long term for the classroom lecture.

So the online education revolution is here. Universities can take an ostrich approach and allow continuing and systematic market incursions from for-profit online operators. Or they can figure out the new online tools for learning and reform their face-to-face course offerings. The reality is that universities cannot ignore the new disruptive online education phenomena.

# 3

# Equal Access to Online Education Will Be a Challenge

*Campaign for the Future of Higher Education*

*Campaign for the Future of Higher Education (CFHE) is a nonprofit organization that advocates greater access to affordable, high quality education.*

*The "promise" of massive open online courses (MOOCs) is to significantly expand access to higher education. However, inequalities in the regular, reliable availability of Internet and digital technologies—known as the digital divide—complicate access to MOOCs among disadvantaged students, particularly minorities and the poor. In addition, mounting research demonstrates that the same students—including community college students and less-prepared students—experience poorer performance in online learning settings and higher withdrawal rates than in face-to-face classrooms. Therefore, the rush to expand access to basic and introductory classes through MOOCs in community colleges and lower-tier colleges and universities is misguided. For disadvantaged students, it may ultimately result in academic failure rather than opportunity.*

In her 2012 TED Talk on the virtues of massive open online courses (MOOCs) Coursera co-founder, Daphne Koller, makes her case by arguing that MOOCs will open up never-before imagined access to higher education across the globe. The "promise" that online learning will dramatically expand

Campaign for the Future of Higher Education, "Promises of Online Higher Ed–Access," http://futureofhighered.org, October 2013. Copyright © 2013 by Campaign for the Future of Higher Education. All rights reserved. Reproduced by permission.

access to higher education is, in fact, at the center of the recent push in the MOOC/Online movement. But is this really the best approach if we are serious about providing quality higher education to underserved students?

*Access is a complex, even slippery, term.*

## Challenges Facing Underserved Students in the US

Population growth in the U.S. is fastest among communities of color. The Pew Research Center projects that immigrants and their descendants will account for 82% of the US's growth between 2005 and to 2050.

Unfortunately, access to higher education for these groups is being blocked. The 2012 report "Closing the Door, Increasing the Gap" documents how budget cuts and policy trends in states across the nation have resulted in students being turned away from community colleges. Gary Rhoades writes,

> Traditionally, our community colleges have been critical portals of entry to higher education for underserved students. They enroll high proportions of Latino/a, African-American, and Native-American students and high proportions of students from lower-income and working class families. It is these students whose futures are being compromised by recent enrollment and curricular trends that are refocusing community colleges on a narrower range of students and educational goals.

Other persistent challenges facing these students include tuition rates rising above the rate of inflation, a decline in the purchasing power of Pell grants, and lagging completion rates compared to their more advantaged peers. Achievement gaps based on socio-economic class and race/ethnicity are well-documented.

Furthermore, underserved students frequently need substantial hands-on non-classroom academic support—e.g., financial aid, advising, counseling, and tutoring services. A national survey of chief academic officers in 2010 suggested that academic and financial support, targeted early warning systems, and transition or bridge programs are critical to improving recruitment and retention of at-risk students.

We know from research that underserved students face extraordinary challenges and need a variety of supports to succeed. Yet online course providers target these very students in developmental and introductory level courses at public state universities and community colleges where less affluent and/or less academically prepared students are more likely to enroll. Do these courses really provide meaningful access to quality higher education for underserved students?

## Asking the Tough Questions

While expanded access and greater equity in educational opportunity must be at the heart of any discussion about the future of higher education, access is a complex, even slippery, term.

For access to be meaningful—and not just an empty advertising slogan—students must have a real chance, if they work hard, to succeed in getting a quality education. We cannot simply give them the "promise" of access.

The subprime mortgage crisis is instructive. Problematic loan practices proliferated for years in part because they were conducted in the name of expanding the middle-class dream of home ownership. No one could disagree with that desirable, over-arching goal, of course; and consequently, few questioned the methods being employed by mortgage companies or the huge profits being made. The results of our failure to look behind the rhetoric were disastrous, both for the nation as a whole and for the lives of ordinary people. The disaster for communities of color was especially profound.

We must do better in American higher education.

Meaningful access to higher education must entail more than the opportunity to enroll in a course just as access to the middle-class dream of home-ownership should have meant more than the opportunity to get a loan and move in for a while.

Are we in the process of creating a similar crisis in higher education in the name of "access"? Will "online everything"—courses, programs, MOOCs, online tutoring, online advisors—offer a kind of subprime education for which we will all pay dearly?

While MOOC providers and "online everything" advocates promise the American dream via access to higher education, we need to proceed carefully. We do all students a disservice if we fail to acknowledge the harsh realities of the digital divide and the online achievement gap beneath the big promise.

## The Digital Divide

The term *digital divide* refers to inequities between those who have regular, reliable access to the Internet and digital technologies and those who do not. Promoters of online courses and MOOCs often act as if the digital divide no longer exists. However, there is substantial evidence that the digital divide remains a reality for the very students that online promoters claim they want to reach—low-income students, students of color, and academically underprepared students.

As of 2012, the United States ranked 14th in the world for broadband access per capita according to data from the International Communications Union. In addition, the U.S. Department of Commerce's 2011 "Exploring the Digital Nation" report reveals that while more households used broadband internet service (68 percent) in 2011, "demographic and geographic disparities demonstrate a persistent digital divide among certain groups." The report continues, "lower income families, people with less education, those with disabilities,

Blacks, Hispanics, and rural residents generally lagged the national average in both broadband adoption and computer use." This stands in sharp contrast to the digital access enjoyed by well-educated middle- and upper-class white households.

---

*There is still a divide between technology-driven educators and the low-income, first-generation college hopefuls they are trying to reach.*

---

Highlights from the U.S. Census Bureau's 2013 "Computer and Internet Use in the United States" report provides even more detailed evidence of the persistent digital divide in our nation:

- In 2011, 76.2 percent of non-Hispanic White households and 82.7 percent of Asian households reported Internet use at home, compared with 58.3 percent of Hispanic households and 56.9 percent of Black households. The report notes that among individuals, "about four out of every ten Blacks and almost half of all Hispanics did not use the Internet in 2011."

- In 2011, only 56.7 percent of individuals living in households with annual income below $25,000 reported having a computer in their household. Where Internet use was concerned, about 86 percent of high income individuals reported connecting to the Internet, compared with 49.8 percent of individuals living in households making less than $25,000.

- Not surprisingly, the educational attainment of the head of household also has a direct impact on computer and Internet use. For individuals with less than a high school degree, slightly more than half (50.9 percent) reported computer ownership and Internet use.

• Of the 16 percent of Americans reporting themselves as "no connectivity" individuals, respondents were disproportionately old, Black and/or Hispanic, low income, and poorly educated.

The implications of these facts for many students and the "access" online learning offers them are clear.

The MOOC provider, Udacity, recently came face to face with the digital divide in their experiment with math courses developed at San Jose State University. Reasons for the abysmal results are complex, but the reality of the digital divide was certainly among them. As *The San Jose Mercury News* reported, "It turned out some of the low-income teens didn't have computers and high-speed Internet connections at home that the online course required. Many needed personal attention to make it through. The final results aren't in yet, but the experiment exposed some challenges to the promise of a low-cost online education. And it showed there is still a divide between technology-driven educators and the low-income, first-generation college hopefuls they are trying to reach."

In the face of failures like the Udacity/San Jose State effort, providers of MOOCs as well as online tutoring and student support systems often claim that the "big data" they collect on student experiences in their online programs will provide them with information necessary to continuously improve their product. One wonders how they can possibly be responsive to the educational needs of students caught in the digital divide, who do not persist in online courses or who cannot enroll in the first place?

Students without broadband access or fast, reliable computers lack the basic technology required of the video-heavy MOOC experience. These students are frequently the ones who need greater in-person support (both in the classroom and without) to succeed once they are enrolled. As a result the for-profit MOOC and other online companies who are targeting underserved students are left with data on the already well-served student and not the students who are most in need of access.

## The Online Achievement Gap

Along with a digital divide, there is growing research showing that these same students experience an online achievement gap.

Although online advocates frequently cite a 2010 Department of Education meta-analysis as evidence that online instruction is "just as good as" on-campus instruction, the generalizations we can draw from that study are seriously limited. For instance, researchers at Columbia University note that only seven of the studies focused on semester-length fully online courses. Of those, only one examined the impact on lower-performing students and found that "the lower one-third of students performed substantially better in the face-to-face setting than in the online setting."

Moreover, results reported in a 2010 study at a large, selective university where students were randomly assigned into online and on-campus sections of a course highlight some striking differences in performance. Among lower performing students, males, and Hispanics, those in the online section scored significantly worse on course assessments than their on-campus counterparts. The study concluded,

... our strongest findings in favor of live instruction are for the relatively low-achieving students, male students, and Hispanic students. These are precisely the students who are more likely to populate the less selective universities and community colleges. These students may well be disadvantaged by the movement to online education and, to the extent that it is the less selective institutions and community colleges that are most fully embracing online education, inadvertently they may be harming a significant portion of their student body.

Other studies demonstrate substantially higher withdrawal rates for community college students in online versus on-campus courses, even after controlling for a variety of demographic factors. This trend can be seen vividly in one study of developmental math courses where withdrawal rates were two to three times higher in the online sections and in another where completion rates were higher in the on-campus (80%) versus the online (61%) sections.

---

*Faculty and nonacademic interaction with students in distance education courses play a critical role in student performance by fostering student-instructor and student-student connections.*

---

More recent research focuses on the experience of large numbers of two-year college students in the Virginia and Washington community college systems. Several key findings should give pause to institutions pursuing MOOCs in community colleges:

- Withdrawal rates were roughly twice as high in fully online courses;

- Regardless of academic subject of the course, demographics, or academic background, students performed more poorly in a fully-online course than in a face-to-face course;

- Students with stronger academic background had only a small dip in performance, while more poorly prepared students had a larger dip;

- Performance gaps (e.g., between white students and students who are members of minority groups) tended to widen in online courses.

Clearly, it is not enough to just promise increased access to higher education through online learning. It is critical to understand what works and for whom. The studies above indicate that, in online learning, there are significant lags in performance for poorly prepared students, males, and students of color.

Again, the story of Udacity's experiment at San Jose State University is a cautionary tale. The abysmal pass rates in the courses should not have been a big surprise. Had planners reviewed the research they might, in fact, have questioned whether their format was pedagogically suited for the targeted underserved and struggling students. As Sara Melnick of the National College Access Network pointed out in commenting on the experiment, "...giving more students access to college classes is not enough. . . . They are more likely to graduate if they have academic support and involvement in campus life."

Research on online teaching and learning also tells us what can improve the chances of student success. Studies show that faculty and nonacademic interaction with students in distance education courses play a critical role in student performance by fostering student-instructor and student-student connections and by creating a sense of community and social presence.

For students of color, academically underprepared, low income, or first generation college students, social interaction is particularly important. One study of California community college courses found that while all students in the online courses paid an "online penalty," Latino students paid the highest price with both lower grades and higher withdrawal rates. The study noted that instructor-student interaction and social presence were key factors shaping Latino students' online experiences.

While the lack of social interaction can hurt students, other research suggests that having an affirming and supportive process initiated by faculty and others can foster academic development, especially for low-income, first-generation college students.

Elisabeth Barnett for example, found that for white, black, Hispanic, and Asian community college students, faculty validation made students want to be more integrated into the institution and, particularly for Hispanic students and for women, to persist in college. Manifestations of faculty caring, she demonstrated, positively affect students' progress and persistence in an ethnically diverse community college setting.

Finally, huge online courses—especially MOOCs–are problematic because they rely on peer and machine grading. This is especially problematic for underprepared students who are less likely to be in a position academically to share constructive feedback with their peers and who are less likely to benefit from the computer-scored adaptive assessments or robo-graded essays that do not provide the feedback needed for improvement and for the development of effective critical thinking skills. Tutoring can help; but again, online tutoring programs are not as effective as in-person tutoring.

## Access to What? Access for Whom?

Distance education in various forms—written correspondence, radio, television, computer, Internet—has existed for well over a century in this country. We have learned a great deal about what works and what doesn't. Real access for underserved students must take into consideration the digital divide and the online achievement gap. It seems self-evident that before we offer online courses to any of our students we must know that they have the technology and expertise to benefit from the experience. Furthermore, instructors must be able to devote attention and to respond to their students in both academic and non-academic ways. Huge courses that inhibit faculty-student interaction and the creation of a sense of community do not work for underserved students.

Research repeatedly demonstrates that online courses work best for students who are academically and technologically well-prepared, mature, and highly motivated. Expanding MOOCs and online student support services for remedial and introductory courses in community colleges and less elite state colleges and universities is misguided at best.

In fact, persisting in this direction can be expected to exacerbate the achievement gaps that already exist and could further cement America's tiered higher education system. We risk creating a system in which the rich on-campus college experience is reserved for the elite while we herd first-generation, low-income students into massive online courses. And we seem prepared to do this even though the value of these courses is questioned by many of the faculty who teach them, by college administrators, and by employers. Students certainly know the difference between a face-to-face class and an online one. As one student from the Udacity experiment commented, MOOCs "feel like a hand-me-down education—'Here, watch this video.'"

The dangers of a two-tiered system make the "online everything" providers' rhetoric about bringing higher education to the masses particularly chilling. For most American students, who are increasingly diverse, low-income, and academically less prepared for the rigors of collegiate study, an uncritical rush to "online everything" may, despite the promise, ultimately provide only access to failure.

# 4

# The Future of Small Private Colleges Is Threatened

*Ry Rivard*

*Based in Washington, DC, Ry Rivard is a reporter for* Inside Higher Ed.

*A growing number of small- and mid-sized private colleges are under distress, experiencing falling enrollment due to declines in the college-age population and competition from public colleges. A sampling of the cuts points to serious challenges that could shut down many of these institutions, entailing large layoffs, poor credit ratings, eliminating or reducing programs, and mergers between colleges. Other outside causes of these problems are declines in high school graduates, concerns about loan indebtedness, reduced government funding, and fewer graduate students. Moreover, private colleges face unique challenges, such as a lack of large endowments, dependence on enrollment for tuition, locations in rural areas with shrinking populations, and the perception of being too expensive.*

Some private colleges that managed to weather the recession are finding new troubles.

So they are announcing layoffs, cutting programs and more. Almost all of these small to mid-sized privates are tuition-dependent and lack large endowments. National declines in the number of traditional college-age population mean students just aren't showing up to privates, which are facing competition from public colleges that are more stable now than a few years ago and the reality that privates cannot afford to indefinitely lure students by cutting prices with generous financial aid packages. And this could become a huge problem.

College presidents, private college trade groups and higher ed consultants blame a confluence of long- and short-term trends for battering some private colleges, particularly the small to mid-sized privates that depend on tuition dollars because they don't have significant endowments.

## A Sampling of the Cuts

It's hard to tell if there is an existential threat brewing that could close a significant number of colleges, as some pundits have grandly predicted. But a sampling of the cuts—primarily driven by falling enrollment—suggests serious challenges for many institutions:

- Midway College in Kentucky is dealing with an 18 percent enrollment drop by laying off "around a dozen" of its 54 faculty, according to *The Lexington Herald-Leader*. It has also eliminated about 16 staff positions. In a recent speech, the new president said the college may try to become a "university," expand internationally and add graduate programs to help it grow.

- Holy Family University in Philadelphia cut 40 staff positions—about 7 percent of the staff—and, partially through retirements, reduced the number of full-time faculty to 81 from 100. The university is also shelving low-demand programs, selling land and dorm units and working on other cost-saving measures.

- Anderson University in Indiana approved a plan to cut 16 of its 400 faculty and staff and end its majors in French, philosophy and theater. Anderson's president blamed a decline in enrollment and said to expect more cuts.

- Wittenberg University in Ohio recently eliminated nearly 30 of about 140 faculty spots—"15 occupied and 14 unoccupied faculty positions"—as part of a $4.5 million budget cut, according to *The Dayton Daily News*.

- Martin University in Indianapolis expected 700 students to enroll this fall but only 522 did, so the university cut 16 faculty and staff positions in October [2013].

- Johnson C. Smith University in North Carolina, which was hit hard by changes to financial aid that hurt its enrollment, laid off 21 staffers, not filling 30 other positions and looking to furlough staff and outsource some services.

- Moody's Investors Service just gave Ashland University in Ohio a poor credit rating and warned it could default because of three years of declining enrollment and a relatively small amount of cash compared to debt.

- Central College in Iowa also got knocked by Moody's last month [November 2012] for a decline in first-year students from 412 in fall 2011 to 309 this year. This decline, the firm said, could cause a $3 million shortfall at Central.

- Moody's put Woodbury University in California on a negative credit outlook after a 22 percent drop in the size of the incoming class created a $1.1 million shortfall.

- Pine Manor, a women's college in Massachusetts has dorm rooms for 600 students but decided to go co-ed and admit male students this summer when enrollment fell to 300.

- Goddard College, a nontraditional college in Vermont, is trying to cut faculty and staff pay to deal with a $550,000 deficit in a budget of less than $13 million.

- Burlington College in Vermont is increasing teaching load and looking to increase enrollment from 190 full-time equivalent students in an effort to become sustainable. The college recently lost three department chairs who left after they were asked to go from full-time to part-time, though the college plans to fill those vacancies.

- Nazareth College in New York has reportedly made unspecified cuts in an effort to come up with about $6 million in savings and $2 million more for student aid. The college's total income in 2011 tax year was about $99 million. Enrollment has fallen about 8 percent since 2000.

- Calvin College in Michigan recently announced a plan "to close current and projected budget deficits by eliminating or reducing programs, cutting staff, and raising revenue through enrollment growth and differential tuition rates," according to state news website MLive.

- Dowling College in New York made cuts and reassignments, which its president called "not significant" but which were reported as part of a "downsizing effort because of declining enrollment and struggling finances" by *Long Island Newsday*.

Some colleges are looking to work together in new ways, another sign of stress:

- St. Bonaventure University and Hilbert College in New York, which began talks earlier this year that could result in a merger of the two Roman Catholic institutions.

- In November, Houghton College in New York and Indiana Wesleyan University in Indiana, which is some 500 miles away, also began talking about a long-distance partnership to allow Houghton, a small private, to offer online courses using resources from Indiana.

- Point University in Georgia and Montreat College in North Carolina plan to merge.

- Johnson University, in Tennessee, and Florida Christian College merged this summer.

---

*I think the truth is it's really not going to get better under the old model.*

---

## Fundamental and Irreversible?

Cuts can be attempts to shore up institutions for a strong future. But some people say something fundamental and irreversible is afoot.

"I think the truth is it's really not going to get better under the old model," said Rick Staisloff, a consultant who is the former vice president for finance and administration at the College of Notre Dame of Maryland.

Houghton President Shirley Mullen said the crisis in higher ed is now of a greater magnitude than any she has seen. "I don't believe there is any going back," she said. "I just don't think that's the case. I think whatever happens going forward is something different than we've seen before—I don't think we know exactly what that's going to look like."

There isn't good real-time data on how institutions are doing. Indeed, some colleges have declined to comment on the extent of their problems to media and yet other institutions may be struggling silently in rural areas without aggressive higher ed reporting. Downgrades by bond-rating agencies tend to attract attention, but institutions in really bad shape that know they can't borrow may not even go in for a review.

But using anecdotes from here and there—like this article does—is dangerous, said Hal Hartley, senior vice president at the Council of Independent Colleges [CIC], which represents many private colleges. "Clearly there are lot of difficult economic pressures hitting all colleges and universities—small and mid-sized private colleges are no exception—and for tuition-dependent colleges like the CIC colleges, enrollment is critical to the overall success and financial well-being of the institution," he said, "but I think it's dangerous to pick one year or a couple of examples and generalize that to broader trends."

## Outside Causes and Unique Challenges

The outside causes of recent troubles are numerous: a decline in high school graduates, worries about loan debt, students looking at college programs that would seem to ensure a job after college, new technology, competition from for-profit colleges, a decline in the amount of government aid, the recent economic downturn, the bond market and, because of some rebounds in the economy, a loss of graduate students coming back to college to get new skills.

Private colleges have their own unique challenges, too: small endowments mean they depend on enrollment to bring in tuition dollars, they have smaller class sizes so they can't subsidize operations with large lectures, they traditionally have mostly tenured faculty, they are often in rural areas with shrinking populations and they are perceived as being unaffordable.

Sister Francesca Onley has been president of Holy Family for 32 years. She said the Federal Reserve's decision to taper a bond-buying program and other uncertainty in the bond market helped force the university's hand, as well as new competition in the market, pressures on Philadelphia high schools and rhetoric from President [Barack] Obama has people reluctant to pay private college tuition. "Mr. Obama should go around and talk about what banks are doing to higher education," she said, instead of talking only about the high cost of college.

---

*From 2010 through 2012, freshman enrollment at more than a quarter of U.S. private four-year colleges declined 10 percent or more.*

---

Holy Family cut costs by shelving low-enrollment programs, laying off employees and working to save money on things like printing and marketing. It also decided to add new nursing and accounting programs and rebrand itself. "We have and stand ready to deal with reality," Sister Onley said. "And I think that's what we did last year: we dealt with realities that we were small, that we had this small endowment, but we had this mission."

Institutions most frequently blame demographic shifts in the country on their woes, but not Holy Family. Pennsylvania is expected to graduate about 6,000 fewer high school students in 2016 than last year. But Holy Family's interim chief financial officer Pat McCormick said that works out to a very small problem for Holy Family—if the university is able to enroll the same percentage of Pennsylvania graduates as it does now.

"I think we're worried about two students," he said. "Given that, if we maintain our market share, we're going to lose about two students."

Other colleges cannot be so optimistic. From 2010 through 2012, freshman enrollment at more than a quarter of U.S. private four-year colleges declined 10 percent or more, according to a recent analysis by *The Wall Street Journal*.

## Why Colleges Fail

Mark Putnam, the president of Central College, did his dissertation on why colleges fail. He said temporary things don't worry him as much as long-term trends. Despite recent enrollment losses that spooked Moody's, Central, which has about 1,500 students, is already looking more than a decade ahead as it plans its future.

Putnam said college leaders need to make sure their institutions don't become too big that they depend on high enrollment or too small that they can't thrive.

"Managing those tolerances within any institution becomes the key work of management, to know there are thresholds of consequence, as I would put it," he said in a telephone interview. "And I as president need to know what those consequences are on the upside as well as the downside."

In a statement, he dismissed the implications of Moody's decision to downgrade Central based largely on its enrollment declines.

"This is not a new phenomenon in the history of higher education, nor are we alone," he said. "What is remarkable is that an institution that has not posted an operating deficit, not tapped any line of credit to support operations and has increased its net assets, improved liquidity and cash position, would be downgraded by Moody's on predictable enrollment fluctuations alone."

The number of graduates in Iowa and the Midwest is projected to remain flat or fall for the foreseeable future, according to a recent report by the Western Interstate Commission for Higher Education.

Nationally, about four in 10 privates colleges now report tuition revenue is not keeping pace with inflation.

## Negotiating Demographic Shifts

Other demographic changes may be particularly challenging for some residential private colleges outside of major metropolitan areas. Some of these institutions are largely white and full of traditional college-age students at a time when demographers predict enrollment growth for part-time students, minority students and students from urban areas. "Historically these are not institutions that have been ... visible in the minority community," said Richard Kneedler, former president of Franklin and Marshall College. "It means when their base shrinks it's really a challenge."

The president of Johnson C. Smith University, a historically black college in North Carolina, has similar worries.

"Watch this space," said President Ronald Carter, "see how predominantly white institutions will struggle if there are fewer white Americans to fill their seats. Will they fill them with international students? How many minority students can they really afford with gap funding?"

Carter said American higher ed needs to negotiate the demographic shift carefully. Minority students are generally coming with less money than white students, so colleges that are trying to plug their enrollment losses with minorities are going to have to find some way to help the students pay. If colleges simply cater only to students who can pay their own way and minorities are shut out, "That's a recipe for civil unrest," Carter predicted.

Carter is particularly sensitive to changes in aid policy at the federal level. He said he had to lay off staff because of sudden changes to the PLUS loan program that hit HBCUs [historically black colleges and universities] hard. Carter scrambled to find institutional and donor-backed financial aid for a few hundred students who were going to have to leave the 1,700-student Johnson C. Smith because of the changes. He managed to keep many of them on campus.

---

*The number of privates that are closing has remained steady—about four a year. The number opening? About three a year.*

---

## Some Worries Yet to Play Out

Some of the larger worries about the health of privates have yet to play out in some data sets, said several private college experts.

Kneedler, who is carefully studying the tax filings of several hundred colleges, said he's seen an improvement in finances at privates since the recession. But that, he said, lags what may be happening now because tax filings come out longer after the budget year. Still, he is not particularly concerned about the mid-sized privates but only the smallest institutions without an endowment.

"I get really concerned when you drop down below 700 (students)," Kneedler said. "There, I think, it's really tough, and I think that's been the case for some time and it's not going to get easier, but I wouldn't ring really loud alarm bells for a school of 1,500."

David Warren, the president of the National Association of Independent Colleges and Universities, said the number of privates that are closing has remained steady—about four a year. The number opening? About three a year.

He said there's no doubt institutions are encountering "whitewater" but they are also adapting. "I think over time you're going to see these institutions reshape themselves in the main and overwhelmingly," Warren said.

McCormick at Holy Family, for instance, said the university is able to launch its new accounting and nursing program only nine months after it decided to enter those markets. That flexibility, he said, does not necessarily exist at larger institutions. Programs like nursing already exist in the area, but Holy Family believes the market is "underserved."

## Forcing Colleges to Do Things They Should Have

Mullen, the president at Houghton, said demographic pinches are forcing the college to do things it might not have done otherwise but that it should have.

First, she had to make choices several years ago, when the college reduced its contribution to employee retirement funds and cut pay for faculty and staff—by as much as 8 percent for top earners. The college has gradually increased pay, but not back to where it was.

Now, through its partnership with Indiana Wesleyan, Houghton hopes to begin an online program of some kind.

Mullen said it's too late for online education to be a short-term cash cow for her college, but with 1,032 full-time students, Houghton doesn't have margin for error if on-campus enrollment falls. Expanding online could change that.

"We believe that to prosper for the long haul we need to have a larger economy," Mullen said. "I think it's way too late to think of online education as an instant revenue generator because so many other institutions are doing that."

Several experts on private colleges said it's time to expect colleges to look closely at new partnerships and even mergers.

Mullen, who said Houghton has no plans to merge, said colleges should team up while they still have strength. "I think if you wait too long you have what in the business world is a takeover more than a partnership," she warned.

Ann Duffield, founding principal of Ann Duffield & Colleagues and a former chief communications officer at the University of Pennsylvania, worries about colleges teetering without a nest egg and unable to invest in their future. Without thinking strategically, they could slip, fall and never get back on their feet.

"I think this is a time in American higher education history where we're really in danger of seeing the disappearance of liberal arts colleges and liberal arts colleges have, in fact, been the backbone of American higher education," Duffield said.

# 5

# For-Profit Motives Threaten the Future of Higher Education

*David Francis Mihalyfy*

*David Francis Mihalyfy is an instructor at the School of the Art Institute of Chicago and doctoral candidate in the history of Christianity at the University of Chicago Divinity School.*

*Profit motives have infiltrated American colleges and universities over the past ten years. Rather than supporting education, research, and resources for students and communities, money has been allocated to the outsized compensation of high-level administrators. For example, at the University of Chicago, President Robert Zimmer has received higher-than-average pay increases—including a 110 percent, $1.76 million pay hike—which could have been earmarked for replacing unstable government grants, funding new construction, or creating an endowment for professorship. Also, high compensation for presidents and provosts costs students, resulting in significant tuition increases and barriers to education. Without a system of checks and balances, institutions like the University of Chicago will continue to stray from their academic missions.*

In his second term, Barack Obama has begun contemplating his legacy and thus his presidential library. At the moment, the leading site contender is the University of Chicago [UChicago], not only the birthplace of [economist] Milton

Friedman-inspired economic deregulation, the "fantasies of the Chicago Boys," but also the Obamas' Hyde Park neighbor and former employer.

Less well known, however, is that UChicago also serves as a window into the fully corporatized future of education, where an unquestioned goal is profit for top staff and the checks-and-balances of the trustee system do not function.

In this future, outsize compensation is hidden by a PR [public relations] machine, funded by growing tuition and debt, and allocated despite questionable job performance. Simultaneously, non-profitable but mission-focused endeavors are sidelined and contracts are given to the institution's claimed guardians.

## Profit Motive's Inroads into American Universities

Over the last decade, profit motive has made significant inroads into the American ivory tower. At universities, money is meant to support a larger social mission, not profit presidents and provosts: ideally, these high-visibility support staff should believe enough in education and research to want any extra resources to go there rather than to themselves. At places like UChicago, however, the ideal of administrative public service has been gradually replaced with that of maximizing short-term self-interest, despite debatable benefits to the institutions and the populations that they claim to serve.

Just as with CEOs [chief executive officers], university administrators' disproportionate pay increases now regularly stand out against news about continuing economic stagnation and budget austerity: the *Chicago Tribune*'s notice of a $90,000 performance bonus awarded the president of the University of Illinois's flagship Urbana-Champaign campus, or successive *Boston Globe* revelations about costly clauses in contracts to a past Brandeis [University] president.

UChicago President Robert Zimmer bests these reports, however. He received four successive years of higher-than-average compensation increases, including an unusual 110%, $1.76 million pay spike that not only brought him from $1.6 to $3.4 million in total compensation, but also the top position in the *Chronicle of Higher Education*'s annual rankings of highest-paid private university presidents. Newly released IRS [Internal Revenue Service] figures now also show Zimmer's post-pay spike compensation is around $1.9 million, double what he made five years ago.

*In terms of compensation-per-endowment, [University of Chicago President Robert] Zimmer [in 2012] had leapt from making eight to seventeen times as much as the president of the world's wealthiest university.*

Until now, the peculiarity of Zimmer's compensation has largely gone unnoticed because his benefits have extended to include personal use of its "News Office"—effectively an in-house PR firm serving top staff but funded with institutional money intended to publicize noteworthy achievements in education and research.

Since the December 2013 *Chronicle* rankings release, UChicago News Office statements successfully deflected scrutiny. At the time, media outlets like the *Huffington Post* observed that Harvard's president made only $899,000—not even noting that in terms of compensation-per-endowment, Zimmer had leapt from making eight to seventeen times as much as the president of the world's wealthiest university.

The explicitly final News Office statement nevertheless asserted that Zimmer's compensation was "consistent with leaders of institutions of similar scale and caliber" thanks in part to "data and guidance from an outside consultant who compares similar roles at 20 peer institutions." UChicago, however, refused to explain specific figures or release the names of the twenty comparable peer institutions. Furthermore, the officials directing the News Office's response were not identified despite multiple informational requests to Zimmer, Vice President David Fithian, Chairman of the Board of Trustees Andrew Alper, incoming Provost Eric Isaacs (former director of Argonne National Laboratories), and outgoing Provost Thomas Rosenbaum (the next president of the California Institute of Technology [Caltech]).

Publicly-available data calls into question the accuracy of the UChicago News Office statement, however. Although the collapse of regular and one-time compensation in IRS-reported figures complicates analysis, as the *Chronicle* has noted, comparison of presidential compensation at the other top twenty private universities by endowment shows that Zimmer's recent 110%, $1.76 million pay spike is an extreme outlier. In both percentage and absolute terms, Zimmer's pay spike is around double all other outliers, which consist of 43–49% and roughly $1 million fluctuations.

Additionally, the $42,000 median compensation increase indicates that Zimmer's $115,000–$320,000 annual pay raises in the prior three years were three to seven-and-a-half times higher than normal.

Beyond the President's office, other administrators have also begun diverting disproportionate amounts of money. Since taking office in 2007, outgoing Provost Rosenbaum has seen his compensation increase 50%—and as he leaves to head up Caltech, he is thus due to take with him $1 million from pay raises. This is even apart from any UChicago-particular increase in administrative positions, which have doubled over the last twenty-five years across US universities and are costing what a senior researcher at the American Institutes for Research terms "just a mind-boggling amount of money per student."

## On Par with Major Expenditures and Costing Students

These levels of administrative compensation have now begun to constitute major annual expenditures on par with allocations more clearly fulfilling UChicago's mission. For example, Zimmer's annual compensation could replace unstable government grants for three to four labs a year instead of having them close ($500,000–$750,000 a year per lab), or go a long way towards construction of an international academic center ($3.45 million) or permanent endowment of a humanities or social science professorship (a $3.5 million gift).

---

*Fundraising operations cannot bring in enough money to keep the credit rating unquestioned, yet compensation of a single person like [university president Robert] Zimmer makes up as much as half of projected major annual operating deficits.*

---

These levels of administrative compensation also come at great cost to students as universities shift to a "fee-for-service" mentality found in businesses. For example, current UChicago undergraduate tuition of $46,386 can pose a significant barrier to some students. Many universities adhere to the "high sticker price, high discount" model, in which tuition from the well-off becomes financial aid and helps the less wealthy. Despite much-publicized financial aid initiatives, however, Chairman Alper was confronted at a public appearance by many student questions about "the rise in tuition prices and lack of financial aid"—and he answered by explaining how high demand for a UChicago education allows for high tuition and how high tuition in turn supports new programs. Students have also started to raise detailed questions about on-campus housing priced significantly higher than that in the surrounding community.

Conversely, UChicago has shied away from needed and feasible but money-losing educational initiatives. Situated in an upscale neighborhood surrounded by urban poverty and epidemic gun violence, its Medical Center closed a money-losing trauma center in 1988 and has since been beset by protests, including one observed by undercover campus police. Official statements, hospital representatives, and Chairman Alper claim that high costs and a lack of resources makes a trauma center unfeasible, but compensation of a single person like Zimmer now approaches the reported inflation-adjusted $3 million annual operating deficit that ended a community resource benefiting both medical students and trauma patients. Apart from any other lines in UChicago's budget, recalibration of multiple administrators' pay would likely provide more than enough money for a trauma center, a more clearly mission-focused expenditure.

---

*UChicago supported the use of Chicago taxpayer money to build a hotel in the trustee-associated Hyatt chain via controversial funds taken away from public schools and city parks.*

---

Concurrently, UChicago has become an "outlier" and "put its credit rating at risk" by taking on debt equal to more than half of its endowment, according to *Bloomberg News*. A leaked financial plan from June 2013 had already indicated that UChicago was on the path to owe three times as much debt as peers like Northwestern. Accordingly, *Crain's Chicago Business* predicted in August [2013] that due to high debt levels "ratings agencies could downgrade the university's credit by as many as two notches." Since then, Moody's and Standard & Poor's have shifted the outlook of its bond rating to negative on three separate occasions in anticipation of a likely credit downgrade. Fundraising operations cannot bring in enough money to keep the credit rating unquestioned, yet compensation of a single person like Zimmer makes up as much as half of projected major annual operating deficits. Nevertheless, UChicago's financial adviser has vouched that "[t]he money is going to . . . programmatic strengths."

## Elites Rewarding Elites

A culture of elites rewarding elites seems to lie behind high compensation, especially since UChicago does not seem to possess a reward structure with "rigorous performance standards," as observed by *Crain's Chicago Business*.

Regarding job performance, Chairman Alper has claimed that "Bob Zimmer's compensation reflects the high degree of confidence the board has in his leadership." Yet, apart from Zimmer's discouragement of transparency and accountability, a group of 108 faculty have questioned UChicago's commitment to academic freedom because the Chinese government funds and ideologically screens language instructors. Recent negative publicity also led to the unexplained teaching reassignment of current economics PhD student and infamous Goldman Sachs trader Fabrice Tourre—a move questioned by students since "courageous" commitment to "freedom of inquiry" necessitates the inclusion of "individuals and ideas that are disliked and heavily criticized."

Similarly, documents suggest that Zimmer or someone close to him began an Administration Building elevator policy where uniformed employees were told to use the stairs when Zimmer was in the building, including a man who had received two hip replacement surgeries. These alleged violations of the Americans with Disabilities and Civil Rights Acts were not taken seriously: the ultimate source of the orders was never identified, despite multiple inquiries to Zimmer, Alper, Provosts Rosenbaum and Isaacs, and Vice President Fithian.

Rosenbaum's job performance has been uneven as well despite high compensation. For example, he first celebrated the allocation of $12.5 million for two childcare centers for parents who can afford $1,100–$1,600 a month for fulltime care as a benefit to "the entire community", then oversaw a response touting more widely available parental resources, including a locked, asbestos-containing equipment room advertised as a lactation site.

Importation of a profit-driven mentality seems directly responsible for these compensation practices. Besides scattered individuals like [New York Times columnist] David Brooks, MBAs [Master of Business Administration degrees] dominate the university's Board of Trustees, which elected as their chairman Alper, a twenty-one year veteran of Goldman Sachs.

Additionally, during the same time period that the Board allocated apparently excessive compensation to administrators like Zimmer and Rosenbaum, at least two trustee-associated companies profited from administrative actions, despite the standard opinion that "colleges should simply not do business with the companies of their board members, in order to avoid . . . appearances of self-dealing and personal enrichment."

Most recently, UChicago supported the use of Chicago taxpayer money to build a hotel in the trustee-associated Hyatt chain via controversial funds taken away from public schools and city parks.

UChicago also awarded campus dining services to the trustee-associated company Aramark despite its persistent difficulties meeting basic contractual obligations; in May 2013, UChicago's Dining Services even announced the allocation of two non-Aramark employees for "increased oversight of Aramark daily operations . . . to ensure food safety standards" after city health inspectors "found mouse droppings in food preparation areas" of undergraduate cafeterias.

## Parallels with the Business World

Overall, then, despite its official classification as a nonprofit educational institution, perhaps the University of Chicago's best parallel lies on the outskirts of the business world, the under-regulated financial sector rooted in what President Obama describes as "huge bets—and huge bonuses—made with other people's money on the line." As in finance, top personnel are guaranteed outsize compensation no matter how the institution fares. As in finance, top personnel are insulated from failure, but the consequences of their decisions fall on other stakeholders—UChicago's students, faculty, and staff, of course, but also the local, national, and global publics who should benefit from its research and resources.

Unfortunately, a lack of checks-and-balances hinders reform of institutions that have strayed from their educational missions. Since the UChicago Board of Trustees appoints the UChicago Board of Trustees, the majority determining its present course will determine its future. Other appointment systems do exist; for example, degree-holding alumni elect one of Harvard's two governing boards.

At universities like UChicago, however, the trustees in question would have to choose to rewrite the bylaws and voluntarily cede power and whatever personal benefits they may be receiving under the current system of governance. Under such conditions, change is very difficult.

Ultimately, higher education's future can be clearly glimpsed through the University of Chicago: power and money are congealing at the top, so that the few increasingly benefit, to the detriment of most.

# 6

# Economic and Racial Segregation Must Be Addressed in Higher Education

*Richard D. Kahlenberg*

*Richard D. Kahlenberg is a senior fellow at the Century Foundation, where he directs its Task Force on Preventing Community Colleges from Becoming Separate and Unequal.*

*While colleges and universities can be credited for educating a more diverse range of students, this encouraging trend is accompanied by increased inequality in higher education. At competitive four-year institutions, high-income students significantly outnumber low-income students, and at community colleges, low-income students outnumber high-income students. Such segregation impacts academic outcomes; strong evidence demonstrates that in economically and racially integrated elementary and secondary schools, all students perform better. Colleges and universities must undertake efforts comparable to those of elementary and secondary schools to bridge the education divide, such as responding to racial and economic stratification and attracting more middle-income students to community colleges.*

Our higher-education system is often thought of as a model for elementary and secondary education because top American universities rank among the very best in the

Richard D. Kahlenberg, "What Colleges Can Learn from K–12 Education," *Chronicle of Higher Education*, May 22, 2013. Copyright © 2013 by Chronicle of Higher Education. All rights reserved. Reproduced by permission.

world. But maybe it's the reverse that is true. After all, only about half of first-time college students earn certificates or degrees within six years, a completion rate much lower than among high-school students. At community colleges, while 81 percent of first-time entering students say they would like to earn bachelor's degrees, only 12 percent do so within six years.

Why are completion rates so low in higher education, especially community colleges? One reason, according to a blue-ribbon panel assembled by the Century Foundation, is that higher education has not directly confronted the growing economic and racial separation of students within its ranks. Largely separate sets of institutions for white and minority students—and for rich and poor—are rarely equal, either in K-12 schooling or in higher education.

---

*Students who attend wealthier and whiter community colleges have higher success rates . . . than those who attend poorer and more heavily minority two-year institutions.*

---

## A Troubling Undercurrent of Increased Inequality

In recent decades, colleges and universities, to their credit, have greatly increased access, educating a much larger and more economically and racially diverse set of students than in the past. But this positive trend has been accompanied by a troubling undercurrent: increased inequality within the higher-education system. According to research by Anthony P. Carnevale and Jeff Strohl, of Georgetown University, fewer high-income students attend community college than in the past. High-income students outnumber low-income students by 14:1 in the most competitive four-year institutions, yet poor students outnumber wealthy students in community colleges by nearly 2:1. Even within the two-year sector, new research for Century's panel finds considerable economic and racial separation and reduced outcomes where segregation exists.

At the K-12 level, substantial evidence has established that all students do better in economically and racially integrated schools than they do in high-poverty schools. Policy makers have put in place two sets of responses. After the 1954 *Brown v. Board of Education* decision, schools took steps to desegregate by race, and more recently have sought to attract middle-class students to urban schools through "magnet" programs. On a parallel track, federal policy makers chose to provide extra funds to high-poverty schools through Title I of the Elementary and Secondary Education Act of 1965. Furthermore, more than two-thirds of all states provide additional funds—most commonly 25 percent more—for low-income students or those in need of remedial education.

By contrast, in higher education, policy makers have adopted modest affirmative-action programs to integrate selective four-year institutions. But there are no comparable efforts to attract middle-class students to community colleges. And there is no higher-education analogue to state or federal policies that provide extra institutional aid to colleges with higher-need students. Quite the opposite, we shower the most resources on the wealthiest college students and the least on the neediest. The federal tax and research-overhead subsidies at Princeton University, for example, amount to about $54,000 per student, according to the economist Richard Vedder.

Economic and racial stratification is familiar but by no means natural, inevitable, or efficient. In K-12 schooling, low-income students given a chance to attend more-affluent schools rank two years ahead of low-income students at high-poverty schools on the fourth-grade National Assessment of Educational Progress. In higher education, studies have found that students who begin at four-year institutions are 15 to 30 percentage points likelier to receive a bachelor's degree (controlling for entering preparation levels) than comparable students who begin at community colleges, where student bodies are poorer.

Moreover, new research from California, commissioned by the Century task force, finds that students who attend wealthier and whiter community colleges have higher success rates (controlling for student preparation at the institutional level) than those who attend poorer and more heavily minority two-year institutions.

Why does economic and racial separation appear to affect outcomes at the higher-education level? For one thing, institutions serving low-income and working-class people generally wield less political power and are shortchanged by legislatures. For example, from 1999 to 2009, operating expenditures per pupil increased by almost $4,200 at public research universities, while public community colleges saw just a $1 increase (in 2009 dollars). Research also finds that the economic makeup of the student body can affect the curriculum offered, the level of expectations that faculty have, and the academic culture.

## Bridging the Higher Education Divide

What can be done? Century's 22-member Task Force on Preventing Community Colleges From Becoming Separate and Unequal, chaired by Anthony Marx, president of the New York Public Library and a former president of Amherst College, and Eduardo Padrón, president of Miami Dade College, sets out a number of recommendations in its new report, "Bridging the Higher Education Divide: Strengthening Community Colleges and Restoring the American Dream."

The group, which is supported by the Ford Foundation, endorses the continuing efforts to expand best practices at community colleges but also suggests that policy makers must go further, taking substantial steps to address racial and economic stratification in higher education and to challenge a system in which two-year colleges are asked to educate those students with the greatest needs using the least funds.

In the short term, the federal government should support research on how much more it costs to adequately educate low-income college students compared with their middle-class peers, an analysis that has been widely conducted at the K-12 level. Likewise, the panel calls for greater transparency in public subsidies of wealthy four-year colleges through tax breaks. In the longer term, the task force seeks the creation of state and federal fund streams for higher education, coupled with accountability for outcomes, similar to those at the K-12 level that support institutions with greater numbers of low-income students.

To reduce stratification, the task force backs policies to attract more middle-class students to community colleges (funds for honors programs, guaranteed transfer to four-year institutions, the ability to grant bachelor's degrees in certain disciplines). For their part, four-year colleges should agree to accept community-college transfers for 5 percent of their junior class and should get public incentives to recruit low-income students out of high school.

Four-year students will benefit from economic and racial diversity, and community-college students will benefit from the political capital and social networks provided by integrated student bodies. These bold steps to bridge the higher-education divide will help colleges strengthen American competitiveness, bolster American democracy, and revive the American dream.

# Community Colleges Will Be an Important Part of Higher Education

*Rob Jenkins*

*Rob Jenkins is an associate professor of English at Georgia Perimeter College and author of* Building a Career in America's Community Colleges.

*The role of community colleges is missing from the discussion surrounding the crisis in higher education. But they are here to stay, excelling in five areas. As engines for workforce development, community colleges offer hands-on technical training that cannot be provided on the Internet or at many companies. They are uniquely structured to recruit and educate remedial and unprepared students. Over a decade, community colleges have also embraced and improved online education, unlike many four-year institutions. Classroom teaching at these campuses is high quality and underrated—taught by the best instructors, not the biggest names. Finally, affordability amid difficult economic times and rising tuitions will keep community colleges viable.*

For all of its holiday cheer, December 2012 also brought a fair amount of doom and gloom. We had the fiscal cliff, the gun-control debate, the Mayan calendar hysteria. And in higher education (speaking of hysteria), we were treated to dire predictions regarding "The End of the University as We Know It," as [author] Nathan Harden put it in *The American Interest.*

Rob Jenkins, "What About Community Colleges?" *Chronicle of Higher Education*, January 15, 2013. Copyright © 2013 by Chronicle of Higher Education. All rights reserved. Reproduced by permission.

Largely missing from the discussion of catastrophic changes facing academe is any mention of how community colleges might fare. Harden argues that residential campuses will basically cease to exist over the next few decades—except, perhaps, at elite universities—replaced by MOOCs [massive open online courses] and other technology-driven forms of mass learning. But he says very little about two-year colleges, except to suggest, briefly, that they, too, could "outsource many of their courses via MOOCs."

(Please note that, for the purposes of this essay, I will use the terms "community college" and "two-year college" more or less interchangeably. But what I'm really talking about is what has come to be known as the "access institution," where students can earn credit toward transfer to a university or can complete two-year degrees or certificates that will enable them to enter the work force. Most of these institutions are still two-year colleges, although many have dropped the word "community" from their name, and some even offer bachelor's degrees.)

---

*Community colleges are, indeed, a powerful engine for workforce development, delivering technical training (and retraining) for thousands of students.*

---

As someone who works in higher education, I must admit that predictions like Harden's always make me a little nervous. This is my livelihood we're talking about, after all. But as a community-college professor, I am reassured by the fact that two-year institutions occupy a unique place in the academic universe, one that might not be filled as easily as some imagine. A couple of years ago, in a speech to faculty members and students at my campus, a visiting dignitary stated that "if Georgia Perimeter College did not exist, someone would have to invent it." I'd like to borrow that phrase and apply it here more broadly to community colleges in general: If they didn't exist, someone would have to invent them.

Specifically, I see five areas in which community colleges excel, and which make it unlikely that they will be disappearing anytime soon:

## Workforce Development and Training

It's true that I have railed in these pages against the tendency among politicians and other decision-makers to view two-year colleges as merely engines for work-force development, ignoring the fact that we also provide a liberal-arts education for nearly half of the college-going population.

But community colleges are, indeed, a powerful engine for workforce development, delivering technical training (and retraining) for thousands of students, enabling them to earn a decent living, and powering the economy in many parts of the nation.

That is an incredibly important function, one that cannot easily be replaced by MOOCs or any other form of mass education on the horizon. Most technical training is by nature hands-on, requiring extensive facilities and on-site instructors. (Honestly, would you want to have your hair cut by someone who learned how to do it by watching the equivalent of You-Tube videos?) Many companies do not have their own training facilities and count on local community colleges to provide skilled workers. That is unlikely to change anytime soon.

## Remedial Education

A recent national report, "Core Principles for Transforming Remedial Education," said: "Half of all undergraduates and 70 percent of community-college students take at least one remedial course."

There is much debate in that document and elsewhere over how many of those students actually belong in remedial courses, but the fact remains that large numbers of students graduating from American high schools (or not graduating, as the case may be) need some sort of remediation. Given the country's shifting demographics and the financial difficulties faced by most school systems, that trend, too, seems unlikely to change—except, perhaps, to get worse.

Many unprepared students will continue pursuing higher education to chase the American dream. And most of them will end up at two-year colleges, because they don't have the grades and test scores to get into four-year colleges, and because—let's face it—two-year institutions are about the only ones actively recruiting remedial students these days. Most four-year colleges have basically given up on them, unless they happen to be athletes.

Even if many institutions end up following the recommendations outlined in "Core Principles"—essentially, that most students who test into remedial courses should be placed instead into college-level courses with "additional support"—that's merely another (if possibly more effective) form of remediation. And once again, community colleges are uniquely structured to provide the kind of intensive, personalized support such students need.

## Online Education

To paraphrase an ad for a fast-food chain, community colleges didn't invent online education; we just made it better.

The fact is, other than for-profit institutions, no other sector of higher education has embraced online learning the way community colleges have. Our motives might not always have been the purest, but we have made a significant commitment to developing our online infrastructure, training online instructors, and recruiting online students. For more than a decade, while our four-year counterparts have dithered over whether to offer this, that, or any course online, community colleges have pushed to provide more and more online options for more and more students.

The result is that we have become remarkably adept at teaching online. More important, we have figured out how to make online courses as personal as possible, which seems to be the key for the vast majority of students. Studies show consistently that one of the main reasons students come to community colleges in the first place is that we offer smaller classes where the instructors know them by name. I believe that holds true for online as well as for face-to-face.

As I've read the comments following articles like "Jump Off the Coursera Bandwagon" and "The False Promise of the Education Revolution" in *The Chronicle*, one thing I've noticed about MOOCs and other such "innovations" is that they seem to appeal mostly to students who are already well educated.

---

*More and more students will be taking courses online . . . [and] most of them will seek out the smaller "classrooms" and more personalized online experience offered by community colleges.*

---

Often those students are either professionals seeking to gain additional expertise in their fields or people looking to expand their intellectual horizons—like the engineer who takes an advanced poetry course just because she likes poetry and didn't have an opportunity to pursue that interest in college.

In other words, these are highly motivated, extremely self-directed learners. But the vast majority of undergraduates who register for online classes are not either of those things—especially in required core courses they don't really want to take. That's why online faculty members at community colleges have worked so hard for years to make their courses as student-friendly as possible.

It may be true, as prognosticators claim, that more and more students will be taking courses online. But if so, I believe most of them will seek out the smaller "classrooms" and more personalized online experience offered by community colleges, rather than the faceless crowds of MOOCs.

## Classroom Teaching

One of the ideas behind the MOOC movement, as I understand it, is that students are better off taking a course from a famous professor at Stanford or MIT [Massachusetts Institute of Technology] than from some no-name instructor (like me).

That reasoning has a couple of obvious flaws. One is that being well known in a particular field doesn't necessarily make someone a great teacher. And the inverse is also true: There are thousands of great college teachers laboring away out there in relative obscurity. Such teachers can be found disproportionately at community colleges.

While "great teaching" may be difficult to quantify, anecdotally speaking, I spent many years as a department chair reviewing teacher evaluations. I was continually struck by how well almost every member of my department fared, and even more so by the students' comments—especially those who had transferred in from four-year institutions and seemed genuinely shocked at the high quality of instruction they found on our campus.

Why is that? Because teaching is what we do. It's what we care most about. It's what we take pride in. When we hire new faculty members, we're looking for the best teachers we can find—not the best researchers or the biggest names. Most of our faculty members have a great deal of teaching experience, because, for better or for worse, we rarely hire people who don't.

Sure, if you love Shakespeare, it might be wonderful to take a course from a famous Shakespearean scholar at one of the world's great universities, even if "taking the course" simply means watching videos on your computer. But all of those students who don't love literature—or biology, or calculus, or whatever—are just looking for a teacher who can help them learn the material and get through the course. And an increasing number of them are looking for those teachers at community colleges.

## Economic Value

The main reason community colleges will remain viable educational options for many years to come is that our institutions are such a great value. In my state, tuition and fees for a full-time student at a two-year college are about a third of what students pay at one of the state's large research institutions, and about half of what they pay at the smaller, regional universities. Many of our students also live at home, which reduces their expenses even more.

Pair that kind of savings in a difficult economy with the fact that students can transfer their credits directly to a university, and it's easy to see why two-year colleges are now enrolling many students who, a decade ago, might have gone off to a regional or even flagship university.

Sure, prestige is an issue, as is peer pressure at the high-school level. It's no fun to admit you are "going to the community college" when everyone else is opening acceptance letters from well-known universities. But as one student told me recently, echoing many of his peers, "So what if I attend GPC [Georgia Perimeter College] for a couple of years before transferring to UGA [University of Georgia]? When I get my bachelor's degree, my diploma will still just say 'The University of Georgia.'"

As long as students are looking for inexpensive courses that transfer easily, with excellent teaching, a supportive environment, and a variety of options—both online and face-to-face—community colleges will continue to thrive. And if they ever, for any reason, cease to exist, somebody will just have to invent them all over again.

8

# Community Colleges Should Be Allowed to Offer Four-Year Degrees

*Robert L. Breuder*

*Robert L. Breuder is president of the College of DuPage, a community college in Glen Ellyn, Illinois, that serves the greater Chicago region.*

*With student debt becoming a $1.1 trillion dilemma, free tuition is a hot topic among policymakers and higher-education officials. For example, Oregon's proposed "Pay It Forward, Pay It Back" plan would do away with tuition, arranging students to pay the state a portion of their incomes after graduation. Nonetheless, instead of sidestepping the issue of tuition costs, the problem should be fixed from the inside out. Allowed in twenty-two states, community colleges should be able to grant four-year degrees. Many offer high-quality, up-to-date academic programs oriented to the job market—without the large tuitions of four-year institutions. Reducing the costs of higher education outright is the best way to eliminate lifelong student debt.*

Free tuition seems to be quite a hot topic in higher education as of late, and with good reason. With increasing tuition costs and fewer options for borrowing at fiscally responsible interest rates, states are feeling the burden of unpaid loans like never before. With student debt in the U.S. surpass-

Robert L. Breuder, "Free Tuition a Debt Solution for Higher Education? Let's Take Action From the Inside Out," *Huffington Post*, June 4, 2014. Copyright © 2014 by Robert Breuder. All rights reserved. Reproduced by permission.

81

ing consumer credit debt for the first time in U.S. history, this $1.1 trillion dilemma has many states taking action to find a solution to the question: How can students obtain higher education, build a career and pay back their loans without it becoming a life-sentence?

## Creative Plans to Finance College

Last summer [in 2013], Oregon took a step toward offering free college tuition when Gov. John Kitzhaber signed a bill ordering a state commission to examine whether free tuition is feasible. The state legislature subsequently passed a bill that could dramatically change the funding of public education in Oregon. The proposed "Pay it Forward, Pay it Back" plan would eliminate tuition completely—instead of paying upfront, students would sign up to pay the state a proportion of their income after they finish college. It will be a few years before anything goes into action, as the bill instructs the state's Higher Education Coordinating Committee to set up a pilot program for consideration by the state's 2015 legislature.

In addition, Tennessee Gov. Bill Haslam signed into law on May 13 [2014] a promise of free community college tuition to every high school graduate in the state. The Tennessee Promise plan, which goes into effect next year, will use $34 million from lottery funds to cover tuition for a two-year degree. Currently one-third of residents in Tennessee have a college degree. Gov. Haslam's plan is to increase this number to 55 percent through this program.

*Tennessee wants to use lottery money to create his state's free community college program for high school graduates.*

This spring, Michigan legislators also hatched a creative plan to finance college tuition. The state's proposed bill would create a pilot program that offers a free education for students in exchange for a fixed percentage of their income—2 percent for community college students and 4 percent for public university students—that would be placed into an earmarked fund for five years for every year they attended school under the program. According to the *Detroit Free Press*, this bill is currently working its way through the Michigan legislature and a hearing date has not yet been scheduled.

Illinois legislators are also getting in on the debate in the form of HB 5323, which would authorize the Illinois Student Assistance Commission to study the feasibility of a program allowing students to attend college and repay their interest-free loan after graduation as a small, fixed percentage of their future disposable income. . . . While the Pay It Forward, Pay It Back Act is an interesting idea, there are upfront costs to offering a multitude of students free education, and repayment likely will take years. A similar proposal in the state of Washington caps the repayment period at 25 years.

## Fixing the Problem from the Inside Out

Given these factors, how then would a tuition-free college program sustain itself? Tennessee wants to use lottery money to create his state's free community college program for high school graduates. Oregon leaders hope their feasibility study determines how much money the program will cost and whether to limit free tuition to recent high school graduates. In addition, Illinois is in a financial crisis now, unable to make its obligations to the pension fund of public education. The annual Illinois Financial Report puts the state's current deficit at $44.79 billion.

And student loans are spiraling out of control. According to the U.S. Department of Education, the number of student borrowers taking the maximum in loans each year—$12,500 for undergraduates—has increased 60 percent in 2008 to 68 percent for the 2011–2012 academic year.

As a community college president for nearly 34 years, my advice to higher education and legislative officials is to stop, step back and, beyond merely shifting the cost of a college education, look at fixing this problem from the inside out.

Aside from free tuition or Pay It Forward programs, let's consider innovations at the community college level that puts four-year diplomas in the hands of our students at a minimal cost. Three years ago, my institution, College of DuPage [COD], the largest community college in Illinois, started a 3+1 initiative that has resulted in offering baccalaureate programs on campus with partner universities at significantly reduced tuition rates. We now offer 12 degrees at COD through five partner universities. Total sticker price? All in, less than $36,000 for the same baccalaureate degree offered at roughly four times that amount at other state colleges in Illinois.

College of DuPage is also pursuing another way higher education can reduce student debt significantly: cut the cost of earning baccalaureate degrees by allowing community colleges to offer them.

According to the Community College Research Center at Columbia University, approximately 45 percent of all undergraduate students—or 8.3 million students—are enrolled in community colleges. College of DuPage and other community colleges provide high-quality, affordable academic programming in line with current job demand and preparing our students for new and emerging fields. We keep up with market trends and look for new ways to educate students and stimulate the economy without the high cost of four-year institutions.

I think our state leaders would be wise to consider allowing community colleges to offer baccalaureate degrees to further assist current and future students. Twenty-two states already do this. Currently, College of DuPage is leading the charge in the state of Illinois to move toward community colleges offering Bachelor of Applied Technology (BAT) and/or Bachelor of Applied Science (BAS) degrees.

Given that community colleges can offer baccalaureate degrees at a fraction of the cost of four-year institutions, it seems to me that reducing a student's cost in the first place is the best step toward eliminating a lifetime of loan repayments. Let's truly pay it forward by fixing this problem properly—from the inside out.

Free tuition seems to be quite a hot topic in higher education as of late, and with good reason. With increasing tuition costs and fewer options for borrowing at fiscally responsible interest rates, states are feeling the burden of unpaid loans like never before.

9

# The Dropout Rate of Community Colleges Is Problematic

*Bob Rath, Kathryn Rock, and Ashley Laferriere*

*Bob Rath is president and chief executive officer of Our Piece of the Pie (OPP), a nonprofit educational organization dedicated to helping urban youth. Kathryn Rock is an external affairs specialist at OPP. Ashley Laferriere is a grant writer at Providence Public Schools and a former consultant at OPP.*

*Dropout rates among community college students are extremely high—less than 30 percent enrolled full-time earn their associate's degree in three years. The road to obtaining their degrees or credentials is more difficult for numerous reasons. Many students are academically unprepared, unable to meet the rigors of college-level coursework. Another problem is remedial education; almost half of community college students are required to take remedial courses, where their time, money, and efforts earn no credits. Also, inadequate financial aid forces them to attend college part-time and work to cover their expenses. Other barriers to graduation facing community college students are a lack of nonacademic skills and support needed to navigate the path through school and the competing obligations of jobs, family, and commuting.*

"*In the coming years, jobs requiring at least an associate degree are projected to grow twice as fast as jobs requiring no college experience. We will not fill those jobs—or keep those jobs on our shores—without the training offered by community colleges.*"—President Barack Obama

The United States economy is expected to grow by 14.4 million jobs between 2008 and 2018, with 97% of these new positions, and 63% of all occupations, requiring a postsecondary credential of some type. With these demands in mind, the US is currently on track to face a shortage of nearly 5 million workers to fill positions that require postsecondary credentials by 2018. Policymakers, educators, nonprofit organizations, and postsecondary institutions, must rise to meet President Obama's challenge of graduating an additional 8.2 million postsecondary students by 2020. We must come together to ensure that college students receive the support and guidance they need so they can succeed in obtaining a postsecondary credential. These graduates will fill tomorrow's high-demand positions and thrive as the workforce of the future.

While job growth for all workers is expected to average 10%, job growth for those with an associate's degree is expected to grow at nearly double that rate, at almost 19%. Job growth for associate's degree holders is expected to even surpass new job growth for bachelor's degrees. Not only will associate's degrees be in high demand, but jobs requiring associate's degrees will offer competitive wages. As recently as 2006, nearly 1 in 6 jobs paying above average wages, and experiencing above average growth, required an associate's degree. In fact, the average expected lifetime earnings for an individual with an associate's degree is approximately $1.6 million, nearly $400,000 more than the expected earnings of a high school graduate.

The workforce demands of the future cannot be met by our current postsecondary education system. To produce the number of graduates necessary to meet the rising demand, community colleges must play a central role and graduate a greater number of students. Because community colleges typically cost less to attend than 4-year institutions, have open enrollment policies, and offer more flexibility than 4-year programs, they offer a feasible path to graduation for many students who may not otherwise pursue a degree.

---

*Between 2003 and 2008, states across the country gave over $1.4 billion, and the Federal government gave over $1.5 billion, to college students who ultimately left school after just 1 year.*

---

## The Community College Dropout Crisis

Reducing the high school dropout rate is a national priority. Youth development organizations, states, and school districts are working tirelessly to develop strategies to help struggling students succeed. Unfortunately, the same emphasis, support, and assistance are not offered to another group of struggling young people: community college students. Too often, student supports stop at high school graduation and community college students are overlooked, despite the fact that dropout rates among this population are extremely high and the economic and social benefits of completion are extensive.

According to Complete College America, less than 30% of students who enroll full-time in community college complete an associate's degree in three years. Completion rates are especially low for minority, low-income, and older students. Just 7.5% of African American students, 11.1% of Hispanic students, 11.8% of low-income students, and 14.4% of students over the age of 25, enrolled full-time, complete a 2-year associate's degree in 3 years. Part-time students complete at even lower rates, with just over 2% of African American students, 2.6% of Hispanic students, and 4.3% of low-income students completing an associate's degree in 3 years.

In Connecticut, the situation is equally dire. According to a 2009 report by the P-20 Council, just 7% to 24% of community college students (depending on the institution) graduate within 3 years of entering school. This means that between 76% and 93% of students are paying 3 years of community college tuition without receiving a diploma as a result of their investment. This wasted tuition money not only affects personal finances, but state and federal funds as well, since many community college students receive student loans to cover tuition costs. In fact, between 2003 and 2008, states across the country gave over $1.4 billion, and the Federal government gave over $1.5 billion, to college students who ultimately left school after just 1 year. Total state expenditures for first year college dropouts in Connecticut topped $62 million between 2003 and 2008. . . . Funds expended can include a combination of personal, state, and federal dollars.

This is not to say that community colleges do not serve an essential purpose, or that investing state and federal funds in these programs is a waste. Graduates of community college produce significant social benefits over non-graduates including, lower unemployment rates, increased tax revenue, and reduced crime rates. In addition, community college provides an affordable, accessible postsecondary option, where young people can acquire the credentials they need to meet labor market demands. As it is estimated that by 2018, jobs requiring an associate's degree will grow at a rate faster than those requiring any other academic credential, improving community college student success rates will not only increase the likelihood of individual student achievement, but save students and taxpayers a significant amount of money in the process. . . .

Graduating from college is difficult; careful study, concentration, and long-term commitment are required to obtain a degree. Because of this, many students struggle to complete their credential. For community college students, the road is often more difficult. Many enter college unprepared or under-prepared for the academic rigor of college level work. Others are shuttled into remedial courses, which often serve as a roadblock to credit-bearing classes and college completion. Still others become lost in the maze of majors, lectures, and high cost. Whether students experience all or just some of these problems, the reasons that many community college students fail to complete their degree must be carefully examined so high-quality solutions can be found to help students succeed.

*Over 67% of African American students, 58% of Hispanic students, and 64% of low-income students pursuing a 2-year degree require remediation.*

## Inadequate Academic Preparation

While more students are attending college than ever before (attendance rates have increased from 49% in 1972 to 69% in 2005) many students are arriving at college without the academic foundation necessary to excel. Weak curricula, unclear standards, and a lack of alignment between high school and college coursework leaves students stranded in college without the academic foundation they need. This is particularly the case under the new Common Core State Standards for English Language Arts and math. These new standards are more rigorous, intended to better prepare students to succeed in postsecondary education. However, schools are struggling to ensure that all students are truly mastering these skills before graduating.

This sets students up for failure, with time and money wasted taking remedial courses to fill gaps in the knowledge they should have acquired while still enrolled in high school. In fact, inadequate academic preparation is a cost that must be paid twice, with taxpayers paying first for students to learn academic material while in high school and again once students are enrolled in college. Student's lack of academic preparation and the need for remediation comes at an estimated national cost of $3.6 billion. Avoiding this path, and improving a student's chances of college success, should start long before students begin college level work. Acquiring a strong academic foundation prior to college is central to a student's successful admission to college and to the likelihood that they will not require remediation once they are enrolled.

Inadequate academic preparation also contributes to one of the most prohibitive factors in a student's ability to complete an associate's degree—the amount of time that they must remain enrolled in college. According to Complete College America, the longer a student is enrolled in school, the less likely they are to finish their degree. Many students cannot afford to attend school full-time, because 75% are working, raising children, commuting to school, or juggling some combination of these three obligations. In addition to personal obligations lengthening their enrollment, students find themselves inadequately prepared for college and, as a result, are forced to take non-credit bearing remedial courses. The combination of outside obligations and inadequate academic preparation is often too much, causing students to drop out.

## Remedial Education

Increased time in school is prohibitive—so much so that it has been shown that the longer it takes a student to complete developmental or remedial education requirements, the less likely they are to remain in school. This is extremely alarming when considered in light of the large number of students required to take remedial courses each year. Complete College America reports that almost 50% of students entering 2-year colleges are required to take remedial classes. This number is even higher for minority and low-income students. In fact, over 67% of African American students, 58% of Hispanic students, and 64% of low-income students pursuing a 2-year degree require remediation.

Despite being noncredit-bearing, remedial courses cost students the same amount as credit bearing classes. Nationally, approximately $3 billion is spent annually on remedial courses, and the cost is constantly growing. According to The College Board, the average tuition at public, two-year colleges increased by just 5% from 1992–2002. Yet, in the following decade (2002–2012), the average tuition at public, two-year colleges increased by 45%. These rising costs are especially disconcerting for remedial students who do not receive credit for their coursework. Students placed in remedial classes can spend thousands of dollars on their education and have no credits to show for their time, money, and hard work.

Remedial education is detrimental not only to students who are required to take these courses, but to state and national economies. Because students who take remedial courses are less likely to complete school the added economic contributions of these potential college graduates are lost. When students enter, but do not complete college, they lose future earning potential, and governments lose future tax revenue.

## Student Financial Aid

While academic preparation for college is essential, adequate preparation does not always translate into successful enrollment and completion of school. In fact, after accounting for differences in academic achievement, a significant gap persists between the percentage of low-income students and high-income students that attend college. Research indicates that low-income high school graduates in the top academic quartile attend college at the same rate as high-income graduates in the bottom achievement quartile. A key factor in this difference is the cost of a college degree and the financial aid available to make college affordable. The bottom line is that college is expensive, prohibitively so for many community college students, especially for students that are low-income.

According to The College Board, the average annual tuition at a public, two-year college, in the 2010 to 2011 school year, was $2,713. This does not include other costs incurred by students such as food, housing, books, and transportation. When these expenses are considered, it is estimated that the average budget required by a community college student is $15,000 per year. This amounts to a significant expense, especially for the many low-income students who often depend on community college to access higher education, and in light of recent changes to Pell Grant funding.

*Many students [who lack non-academic skills] are impacted at the very start of the college process, even before they enroll, when they must take concrete steps to explore college and financial aid options.*

In 2011, the number of semesters in which student could receive a Pell Grant award was shortened from 18 semesters to 12 semesters. This change was implemented in 2012 and, according to the Association of Community College Trustees, is expected to impact 63,000 Pell Grant recipients. This modification is especially detrimental for the community college student population, since Pell Grants typically cover a higher proportion of a community college students' tuition than other college students. In addition, many community college students take longer to complete their degrees than students at 4-year colleges. In fact, 40% of students are only able to attend school part time. This extends the amount of time it takes for students to achieve their degree and the amount of time they require the assistance of a Pell Grant. Now, with fewer semesters of Pell eligibility, these students must receive better supports to ensure that they can get through a degree program.

While this is an issue facing students who apply for Pell grants, many students and families are not even aware of the financial aid that is available. They often overestimate the cost of college and do not know about financial aid options. This problem is particularly prevalent among low-income students and families who are also often deterred by the Free Application for Federal Student Aid (FAFSA). As a result, many students fail to complete the FAFSA, miss important filing deadlines, and lose out on aid that could help them afford college. This forces them to take on work obligations, oftentimes lengthening their time in school, or deterring them from enrolling entirely. Whether due to inadequate financial aid information, rapidly rising costs, or a financial aid system that is complex and confusing, student financial aid plays a key factor in why students leave, or fail to enter, college.

## Lack of Non-Academic Skills

To achieve success in college, students need more than just academic skills. They must adapt to new expectations, learning styles, professors, and surroundings. They must learn to collaborate with new students, and satisfy college course and graduation requirements. For many community college students, these new responsibilities can be overwhelming. This is because many students lack the essential non-academic skills necessary to tackle college challenges. In fact, even students that are deemed *academically* college-ready, through test scores or the completion of developmental coursework, often fail to complete their degree. Clearly, academic preparation influences college success, but it is certainly not the only success factor.

Professors and peers expect community college students to meet certain non-academic behavioral standards, such as navigating complex bureaucratic requirements, utilizing good study habits and time management strategies, and engaging in new kinds of social relationships. These standards are often left unspoken and unwritten, leaving students that lack these non-academic skills, unsure or unaware of expectations. The lack of clarity regarding non-academic skills is particularly detrimental to first-generation and older college students, who make up a large portion of the community college student population. Because non-academic preparation and support for college often depends on parents, teachers, guidance counselors, and other supportive adults with college knowledge and insight on how to succeed, students without access to these adult guides are often left behind. For many first-generation and low-income community college students, support for non-academic skills is simply not available.

A lack of non-academic preparation and support can undermine college student success at any point. Many students are impacted at the very start of the college process, even before they enroll, when they must take concrete steps to explore college and financial aid options. Other students make it to college, but receive negative feedback, poor grades, and experience discomfort on campus, causing them to ultimately drop out. While many community colleges have some type of orientation program in place to combat potential confusion, explain college policies, and highlight support resources, just 38% of colleges report instituting mandatory orientation programs. In fact, after three weeks of college, approximately 19% of entering students are still unaware of their school's orientation program. Skipping orientation can be especially detrimental to students lacking non-academic skills, as orientation provides a valuable opportunity for them to understand how their school works and begin forming new relationships.

## Competing Obligations

Many community college students face significant obligations outside of the classroom that make it difficult to persist in school and concentrate on completing their degree. Work and family life demands are perhaps the most influential among the challenges that community college students face. Because many students have jobs, children, and a commute to school, they are more likely than their 4-year college peers to have poor academic outcomes and, ultimately, drop out. It is critical that students feel connected to their school, and supported by their environment in order to combat these competing obligations and persist in the face of obstacles that threaten to derail their success.

Community college students work a substantial number of hours to support themselves, their education, and their family. According to a study conducted for the Bill & Melinda Gates Foundation, working and going to school simultaneously is the number one reason students provided when asked why they left school. In fact, 60% of community college students work 20 hours a week, and 25% work 35 hours a week. The stress of going to college while working is often too much, causing students to drop out before completing their degree.

Many students work while enrolled in school because of the high cost of postsecondary education. While college costs have risen over 400% in the past 25 years, median family income has only increased 150%—not enough to keep pace. This leaves many families unable to contribute to their children's education, forcing students to work while enrolled in school and resulting in poor outcomes. In fact, research has found that 6 out of 10 students who leave school had to pay for college themselves, and could not rely on support from their families.

Students leave school for a variety of reasons. Whether due to inadequate academic preparation, insufficient financial aid, underdeveloped non-academic skills, or competing life obligations, young people need help to reach their postsecondary goals. With the problems identified, we can begin to develop sound strategies and supportive solutions to improve student success.

# 10

# Tuition-Free Higher Education Must Be Offered

## Richard Eskow

*Richard Eskow is a senior fellow at the Campaign for America's Future, a progressive political organization, and host of the radio news show* The Zero Hour.

*It is only a matter of time before the United States begins to question how a young person can be morally denied a higher education. Statistics show that barriers to a degree are an economic burden. Social mobility is nearing an all-time low, education is becoming an inherited privilege, and the rising costs of higher education unfairly impacts lower-income groups. Additionally, young Americans are falling behind in education among developed countries, tuitions are extremely expensive, and state funding is shrinking. Free higher education, nonetheless, can be affordably achieved in several ways, such as through increased, better-coordinated government spending and ending corporate tax loopholes. Higher education is essential for Americans to fully participate in democratic life.*

Social progress is never a straightforward, linear process. Sometimes society struggles to recognize moral questions that in retrospect should have seemed obvious. Then, in a historical moment, something crystallizes.

Slavery, civil rights, women's rights, marriage equality: each of these moral challenges arose in the national conscience before becoming the subject of a fight for justice (some of which have yet to be won).

I believe the moment will come, perhaps very soon, when we as a society will ask ourselves: How can we deny a higher education to any young person in this country just because she or he can't afford it?

The numbers show that barriers to higher education are an economic burden for both students and society. They also show that the solution—free higher education for all those who would benefit from it—is a practical goal.

But, in the end, the fundamental argument isn't economic. It's moral.

## The College Cost Crisis

Consider the situation in which we now find ourselves:

*Social mobility in the United States is at or near its lowest point in modern history.* A nation which prides itself on the "only in America" myth has fallen far behind other countries in this, the primary measurement of an equal-opportunity society.

In the midst of this class ossification, higher education remains a powerful tool for social mobility.

*Education is in danger of becoming an inherited privilege.* The greatest predictor of a child's likelihood of graduating college lies in the answer to the question, Did his parents graduate high school? The OECD [Organisation for Economic Co-operation and Development] found that "The odds that a young person in the U.S. will be in higher education if his or her parents do not have an upper secondary education are just 29%—*one of the lowest levels among OECD countries* (emphasis ours)."

That's not a "land of opportunity." This kind of economic aristocracy is fundamentally un-American. And it's getting worse.

*The cost of higher education is hitting lower-income Americans the hardest.* As a recent analysis (from the Hechinger Report, in collaboration with Education Writer's Association and the Dallas Morning News) showed, "America's colleges and universities are quietly shifting the burden of their big tuition increases onto low-income students, while many higher-income families are seeing their college costs rise more slowly, or even fall."

---

*The U.S. ranks 14th in the world in the percentage of 25-34 year-olds with higher education (42%).*

---

More student aid is being directed to wealthier students, further exacerbating the educational inequality problem.

And we certainly don't have an overabundance of graduates. In fact . . .

*Young Americans aren't as educated as the young citizens of many other developed countries.* The OECD also found that "The U.S. ranks 14th in the world in the percentage of 25-34 year-olds with higher education (42%)." When all adults of working age are considered, the U.S. is still one of the highest-educated countries in the world. But when this age group is considered, we are falling behind.

That's a personal loss for our young people, and an economic loss for the country. *Better-educated adults earn more*—a lot more. College-educated men in the U.S. earn an average of $675,000 [more] over the course of a lifetime than those with no upper secondary or higher education. That figure is $390,000 for women—and closing that age gap is another moral issue. What's more, the value of a college education *increased* in the U.S. in the first decade of the 21$^{st}$ century.

*Unfortunately, higher education is extremely expensive in the United States.* In fact, the cost of the education itself may be the highest in the world, since other nations include the cost of income lost during the college years. Even when the statistics are combined, only three countries are costlier.

That figure becomes even worse when we consider the fact that, compared to other nations, *public funds pay for far less higher education in the U.S.*. The "Education at a Glance" study also found that "Across all OECD countries, 30 percent of the expenditure on higher education comes from private sources, while in the U.S., 62 percent does."

Or, to put that another way, public funds pay for 70 percent of higher education on average in developed countries. In the United States, they only pay a little more than half as much on a percentage basis—and our education costs more, too.

*The states are withdrawing their education funds.* This trend has been exacerbated as states (the primary source of public higher education) withdraw their funding for public education in times of economic downturn, and fail to restore it in times of economic growth.

Everyone should want to change these statistics. Is that practical? The answer may surprise some people.

## Investing in Education

*Higher education is a very good investment.* The United States has one of the highest "rates of return" on college degrees in the world. OECD data shows that the "net present value" of a higher education—its estimated long-term value, minus total costs—is higher in the United States than it is anywhere else in the world except Portugal.

*Free higher education is an affordable dream.* As Jeff Bryant of the Education Opportunity Network points out in his "free public higher education" petition, free higher education is not an unaffordable fantasy. If public colleges and universities were to be made available to qualified students without charging tuition, the total cost would be an estimated $62.6 billion. And, as [fellow at the Campaign for America's Future] Richard Long notes, approximately $69 billion is spent each year on government aid to students.

There is some overlap between the two figures. Some of that student aid goes to tuition for public colleges and universities. But much of it goes to private universities, at levels of quality that range from Ivy League elite to fly-by-night predatory.

---

*We are currently spending nearly $70 billion per year in student aid.*

---

*Let's not kid ourselves: Doing this the right way would require increased government spending.* It would also call for better coordination between state budgets and federal expenditures, which can be achieved in a number of ways. But it would be money well spent. Higher income for individuals equates to higher spending, and therefore to economic growth.

What's more, debt is also an enormous drag on the economy. *We are currently experiencing a student debt crisis of vast proportions—and it's getting worse.* Federal Reserve data tables show that the total student debt outstanding in this country is now $1.225 trillion. What's more, that figure has risen by nearly $400 billion over the last four years [since 2010], or nearly a hundred billion dollars a year.

*Imagine the stimulus effect that $400 billion might have had in these post-financial crisis years.* Imagine the even greater stimulus effect that we might have experienced if there were a massive write-down on the overall $1.2 trillion. That kind of policy initiative should also be on the table.

How much will it cost? We can't know. We are currently spending nearly $70 billion per year in student aid. Even if that figure were to double—which is by no means inevitable—*it would be more than paid for by Rep. Jan Schakowsky's Fairness in Taxation Act*, which increases tax rates for millionaires and billionaires on a graduated basis to a modest top rate of 49 percent for billionaires. (It was 91 percent under Republican President Dwight D. Eisenhower.) That bill would raise $872 billion over a 10-year period.

*Another way to cover the cost is by closing corporate tax loopholes.* That would bring in an estimated $1.24 trillion over the next 10 years.

Going forward, a system of free higher public education would eliminate the lion's share of student indebtedness. Billions in new funds would return to general circulation each year. Graduates would earn higher incomes, unencumbered by debt. It would be a win-win.

## The Moral Imperative

Economically, free public higher education is an achievable goal. And one wonders why the deficit scolds, who profess such concern for young people in there trying to cut Social Security, seems so disinterested in helping them get an education, find jobs, or fulfill their destinies.

But the fundamental argument in its favor is moral, not fiscal. That moral imperative becomes even stronger when we consider the massive injustice we have perpetrated by forcing graduates into an economy that has reached historically awful levels for new entrants into the job market. That alone is an abandonment of our national obligations—both to young people and to our future. Compounding that misery with record-high student debt is nothing short of disgraceful.

Free public higher education is a clean and ethical solution. Elite private institutions will undoubtedly survive, and there's no reason why grants might not be offered in certain cases for students who can only receive the education they need in specialized institutions. At the other end of the spectrum, many of today's diploma mills would undoubtedly go under. But that, by all the evidence, wouldn't be a loss and might even be a net social gain.

But, while the economic arguments are impressive, it's important not to base this debate on numbers alone. The 2012 platforms of both political parties argued that education initiatives must be geared toward teaching skills that will get graduates hired by America's corporations. That's certainly valuable for students who have chosen that as their educational goal.

The American educational tradition has never been strictly utilitarian. Public institutions of higher learning shouldn't exist merely to provide free employee training for the private sector.

Colleges and universities must also produce the musicians, writers, philosophers, scientists, and visionaries of tomorrow. We must stay true to the vision of educational philosophers like John Dewey, who recognized that the primary purpose of education at all levels is to produce fully realized citizens in a democratic society.

The ability to participate fully in all aspects of democratic life has always been the American dream. Free higher education is essential to realizing that dream, and it's an idea whose time has come.

# 11

# A Proposal: Five Federal Universities

*Freddie de Boer*

*Based in West Lafayette, Indiana, Freddie de Boer is a doctoral student studying rhetoric and composition at Purdue University.*

*To attract the best students, many universities spend money on facilities and extracurricular activities instead of instruction quality, which contributes to the tuition crisis. To make universities compete on price while offering quality instruction, a system of no-tuition federal universities—five for each major region of the United States—should be established with government funding, charitable support, and policies against extravagant amenities. Instead of fancy dorms, endless campus services, or big-name athletics, students would get excellent teaching and valuable professional and personal development for much less than the tuition of many institutions. The out-of-control cost of higher education is a great moral challenge, and thus the return of great, affordable universities is worth fighting for.*

Colleges (and by that I mean their administrators) are desperate to attract the students with the best high school portfolios. But unfortunately, high school students are not that moved by the abstraction of instruction quality. They are, instead, largely moved by the tangible "ooh" factor of dorms, gyms, and dining halls. That's what the internal research of a lot of colleges says, anyway. It's kind of amazing that these

Fredrik de Boer, "My Dream: Five Federal Universities," *L'Hôte*, May 23, 2013. Copyright © 2013 by Fredrik deBoer. All rights reserved. Reproduced by permission.

young people (many of whom I've worked with) are so mercenary in pursuing getting into an elite college and so systematic in their applications, and yet can make decisions based on such ancillary reasons. But then again . . . they're 18 years old. Asking them to not just make major life choices but to make ones that specifically require delaying gratification and choosing fiscal sobriety over prestige is a recipe for unhappiness.

Perhaps what's really irrational is having this massive system that depends so much on the whims of teenagers. But listen. There is rational assessment and then there is irrational panic, and when it comes to discussion of college there's far too much of the latter. As [writer] Noah Millman says, things that are unsustainable won't be sustained. Reform is possible, and indeed, is far more likely than the doomsday scenarios announced by those who are typically animated by anti-academic resentments.

## Universities Must Compete on Price

So how to address the problem? I've made some arguments before about what individual schools can do, and I think they stand up to scrutiny. But we've got to look at some structural changes. The bottom line is that while a university shouldn't be run like a business, and can't if it's to fulfill its fundamental mission, universities have to compete on price for the good of everyone.

---

*Here's my dream: a system of five federal universities. Northeastern American University, Southeastern American University, Central American University, Southwestern American University, and Northwestern American University.*

---

I'm not going to address the MOOC [massive open online course] argument here, largely because it's not my focus here, but also because the MOOC argument is so empty as an argument. It's the ultimate example of The Borg Complex; so often, I interact with people who express no coherent argument beyond "it is inevitable." MOOC discussions have frighteningly little to say about if they *work*, don't reflect on the rampant potential for cheating and fraud, and don't recognize that most undergraduates have no interest at all in living in their parents basement's for their college years. MOOCs can be a great resource for nontraditional students. Anyway. "There is absolutely no inevitability as long as there is a willingness to contemplate what is happening."

The first thing: uncapped student loans need to go. The sentiment is noble; the results, terrible. As long as there's loose money tied to the impulse control of people in their teens and early twenties, people are going to find themselves under mountains of debt. As long as students can borrow, colleges have no direct incentive to compete on price. I know: our message has been the sitcom family fantasy of "you can go anywhere you can get into." That just doesn't fly anymore. Yes, it's nice to go to an expensive university, just like it's nice to have a luxury car or a nice house. It is not responsible for government to help people go into debt to buy luxury items.

Second: the states have to start funding public universities again. The cuts in the last decade have been incredible. The states are good about expressing pride in their universities, but pride doesn't pay the bills.

## A System of Five Federal Universities

If the state U's can claw some funding back and compete on price, that's a big start. But we should make the competition to lower costs while providing quality instruction even fiercer. Here's my dream: a system of five federal universities. Northeastern American University, Southeastern American University, Central American University, Southwestern American University, and Northwestern American University. They would be explicitly oriented towards providing a cheap, quality education in the traditional sense. I'd like to shoot for a tuition of $0, and I think that is a achievable goal with the right governmental funding, charitable support, and ruthlessness about unnecessary amenities. I would settle for $2,500 a year for any student from within each geographical region and $5,000 for any students who want to go to a university from outside of their region.

Here's the bargain students make. . . . No vortex pool; no sushi chefs in the dining hall; no dorms designed by [architect] Frank Gehry. You'll get what you need. We'll have computer labs, but they won't be at every corner of the campus like they are in most. Your dorms will be like dorms from the seventies: utilitarian, not very big, but serviceable and homey. And, sorry: you don't get the truly endless amount of student services on offer at most colleges now. That set of clubs and activities and events that could fill a phone book, we don't have that here. Not just because they cost money in and of themselves but because they take *staff*, and a huge part of the current tuition crisis boils down to the explosion in administration. You can organize clubs and activities and we'll give you spaces in the common areas to do them, but it's gonna be a shoestring affair. You'll have to make things work with your own fundraising and effort. Intramural Ultimate Frisbee sounds doable. Intramural crew does not.

And I'm afraid you're going to have to settle for intramural and club teams you can cobble together, because there will be no NCAA [National Collegiate Athletic Association] varsity sports in this university system. None. Sorry. Despite what most people think, college sports are a money loser for the vast majority of schools. And getting new teams up and running would be even more needlessly expensive. No giant stadiums, no rooting for the old college team. Can't afford it. Can't afford it!

## What Students Do Get

So if they're giving up these things, what do they get? They get a school that is dedicated to providing excellent teaching and career and personal development at a tiny fraction of the cost of many major universities. They get a university system that believes that the actual education should represent the value of attendance, not the name on the degree. They get an education that is based on the idea of personal growth, not on "having an experience," which is best left to Disneyland. More than anything, they start their adult lives equipped with knowledge and skills (having had fun!) without the crushing debt that so many others have faced.

---

*Many people are deeply committed to the fundamental job of the university: to create and house knowledge, skills, insights, and ways of knowing, and to share those with people who want to learn.*

---

The bargain with faculty is easier. The academic job market being what it is, there's tons of published, talented people who are eager to teach and research who would leap at the chance. Here's the case we make. Six figure salaries are not in your future here. (Most humanities and social sciences profs are laughing out loud at that, as that wasn't in the cards for them anyway, but for some in the STEM [science, technology, engineering, and mathematics] disciplines, it's a legitimate concern.) You don't get the gleaming palaces. The amenities available to you will not be equivalent to what people at many schools get. That is a special concern for those in fields with major physical and infrastructural research needs. What you get, instead, is a university where the faculty are still the heart of the university. You won't feel outnumbered by administrators, or feel like you've become a cog in a machine you don't control. The faculty senate will be able to effect real change in policy. You're not going to find your control over essential university functions increasingly being taken by miscellaneous admins.

I genuinely believe that there are many fantastic faculty members who would want to be a part of a university system like this.

The discussion of teaching versus research in the contemporary university is complicated, and I don't want to go too into depth about it here. I do think, in broad terms, that the dilemma is a false one. It is the case that in my fantasy university system here, in order to maintain a commitment to tenure-track faculty teaching as large of a percentage of the classes as possible, professors will have to teach a somewhat larger load than those at R-1 universities. It's also true that, in an effort to keep administrative costs low, many jobs previously done by faculty members will have to be taken up by them again. I believe that there is a balance that can be struck where faculty are given credit for research and given opportunities like sabbatical to undertake it, while maintaining the focus on teaching. I also believe that it's perfectly legitimate for individual universities to develop research, teaching, and administrative tracks within their professoriate, and that compensation and benefits can be tweaked in a way that makes all three of these necessary elements respected and valued within the school.

## An Idea Worth Fighting For

We're living in a time of deep anti-academic sentiment, some of it fair, much of it not. What I observe in my daily life and want to share with others, more than anything else, is just how many people are deeply committed to the fundamental job of the university: to create and house knowledge, skills, insights, and ways of knowing, and to share those with people who want to learn, so that they might better themselves and their society. I will fully admit to a deep and abiding romanticism towards the university. But then I should. Because while I have seen the worst of the academy, I have also seen the best, and I believe in what it can mean for individuals and for our society.

The dramatic increase in tuition, the collapse of public funding, and the attendant rise in crushing debt represent one of the great moral challenges of our lifetime. That challenge can be met, with dedication and with a commitment to the great tradition of societal investment in education and self-improvement. All of us who consider ourselves academics have a deep and personal responsibility to helping college students to graduate with the prerequisite skills and knowledge, and to do so without permanently damaging their economic future. I know of no academic I talk to regularly who does not lament the spiraling costs of college attendance. But we have little direct control. We have to confront this problem through politics, through charity, and through private responsibility. It is possible. This country once had great universities that could deliver education without incurring great costs. It can again, if we work for it. The university, at its heart, is a community of teachers, students, and administrators. That community can represent a great benefit to all involved. It's an idea worth fighting for.

# 12

# Accreditation Should Be Reformed in Higher Education

*Lindsey Burke and Stuart M. Butler*

*Lindsey Burke is a Will Skillman Fellow in Education in the domestic policy studies department at the Heritage Foundation. Stuart M. Butler is director of the Center for Policy Innovation at the Heritage Foundation.*

*Facing the unaffordable cost of a traditional college degree, higher education in America is on the verge of change. One barrier to its transformation is accreditation, the "seal of approval" given to colleges and universities. However, the system is problematic, favoring costly business models for higher education, rating entire institutions rather than courses, and restricting federal aid to students who only enroll in accredited schools. To ensure that higher education keeps pace with the economic future, accreditation should be reformed in numerous ways by policymakers, state leaders, and businesses, such as permitting all institutions to accredit courses, separating accreditation and federal funding, and discouraging it from stifling new ventures in higher education.*

America's system of higher education is on the verge of dramatic change. After years of debate, enterprising academics may have resolved higher education's most frustrating dilemma: the fact that although a college degree or an equivalent set of skills is essential for a good job and the chance of

Lindsey Burke and Stuart M. Butler, "Accreditation: Removing the Barrier to Higher Education Reform," *Backgrounder*, no. 2728, September 21, 2012. Copyright © 2012 by The Heritage Foundation. All rights reserved. Reproduced by permission.

upward economic mobility, a traditional college education has become unaffordable for many Americans—unless they are willing to incur enormous debt. In fact, over half of all graduates with bachelor's degrees incur an average of $23,000 in debt, and cumulative student loan debt now exceeds credit card debt.

Entrepreneurial educators are attempting to resolve this dilemma by using new business models and new ways of learning, such as online courses, to slash the cost of a college-level education. These innovations offer the prospect of a fundamental restructuring of higher education with a sharp reduction in costs—a revolution that would be a boon to students seeking to acquire the skills they need in today's economy.

## The Obstacle of Accreditation

Despite the promise presented by these innovations, a considerable obstacle remains: accreditation. A feature of the traditional education system, accreditation is a "seal of approval" granted to institutions of higher education and is intended to assure students that colleges and universities meet certain standards of quality. And yet, as a system of quality measurement, accreditation is riddled with problems. For example, it favors existing expensive business models for higher education, thereby making it difficult for new models to emerge. Additionally, accreditation rates entire institutions—rather than specific courses—and, as a result, is a poor indicator of the skills acquired by students.

Accreditation also narrows the number of educational opportunities available to students: In order to receive federal student aid, students must attend an accredited school. While accreditation is technically voluntary, students at an unaccredited college are ineligible for federal student loans and grants. Consequently, as federal student aid and subsidies have become an increasingly larger share of university budgets over the past four decades, most institutions have little choice but to seek accreditation.

Without question, America's system of higher education needs dramatic and lasting reform. Accreditation, however, continues to impede such a transformation. If higher education is to keep pace with the demands of future economies, the metrics used to value an education must place a greater emphasis on rating and credentialing specific courses and acquired skills, not institutions. This reform can and should be driven by the private sector so that the skills students receive are the same tools valued by employers. Policymakers, lawmakers, and business leaders need to resist the efforts of existing institutions of higher education to thwart this necessary change.

## What Needs to Be Done

*Federal Policymakers.* Federal policymakers should work to limit Washington's intervention in higher education—specifically, through accreditation—so that reform can take place. Specifically:

1. *End government sanctioning of accrediting agencies and allow any institution to accredit courses.* At the same time, accreditation should be voluntary, and accrediting entities' reputations should rest with market forces, not government institutions. The abundance of online information, coupled with the self-interest of students to be competitive in the job market, "reduces the problem of fraudulently low-quality education to one of *de minimis* proportions."

2. *Avoid federal "scorecards."* A seductive idea, even among some critics of today's accreditation system, is to have the federal government replace or supplement federally driven accreditation with a scorecard that seeks to mea-

sure the output of colleges by criteria such as graduation rates, employability of graduates, and value for money. Such federal intervention would be a mistake: Existing institutions that are comfortable within the cocoon of protectionist accreditation would lobby hard, and no doubt effectively, for output measures that define success in their own terms. Moreover, a competing range of such private outcomes-based scorecards already exists, sponsored by such bodies as *U.S. News & World Report*, *Forbes*, the American Council of Trustees and Alumni [ACTA], and *Kiplinger's*.

3. *Decouple accreditation and federal funding.* ACTA notes that once accreditation agencies became the gatekeepers for federal funding, "accreditors essentially gained regulatory control over colleges." Federal policymakers should therefore decouple accreditation and federal funding through amendments to the Higher Education Act, thus eliminating the necessity that colleges get accredited by the government-sanctioned system. This reform would allow independent accrediting institutions to enter the market, thereby providing students with numerous options for creating their "degree" and shaping their college experience.

*State Leaders.* With regard to reforming the accreditation system, state leaders also have an important role to play:

1. *Encourage investment in 529 college savings accounts.* 529 college savings plans are tax-advantaged accounts that offer an attractive vehicle for families to save for future higher education expenses. Interest earned on money invested in a 529 account is allowed to accrue free from federal income tax obligations. While this is codified in federal law, most states offer either tax credits or deductions to encourage saving in a 529 college savings plan. Many states allow college savings to accrue in 529 ac-

counts without requiring investors to pay state taxes on interest earned and permit families to withdraw money tax-free to pay for tuition, books, and other education-related expenses. Today, at least nine states still subject 529 earnings to state taxes. To provide students with increased flexibility in their higher education financing, those states should allow interest earned on 529 college savings accounts to accrue free from state income tax liability.

2. *Shift state schools to a competency-based model.* Governors and state higher education system leaders should follow the lead of Wisconsin and move state colleges and universities to competency-based degree models. Degrees should be awarded for competency in a given subject, not for the number of hours spent in the classroom. Such a shift would, in turn, expedite degree completion and save money for students and taxpayers alike. Governors should take the lead in encouraging state school trustees to embrace competency-based degrees.

3. *Offer dual enrollment options.* States should offer and expand dual enrollment programs that give advanced high school students the opportunity to take college-level courses while in high school and receive college credit for successfully passing those courses.

*The Business Community.* To be successful, many of these reforms require support from the business community. The business community can help to enhance competition and accelerate reform in two important ways:

1. *Discourage government from using accreditation as a barrier to new higher education ventures.* Successful American businesses understand the value of competition and the need to prevent government-backed regulation or "standards" from blocking new entrants to a market. As

competition increases, existing colleges and universities will attempt to use accreditation to obstruct new business models and to restrict aid to students attending traditional colleges and universities. Recognizing the dangers of anti-competitive practices, business leaders need to get off the proverbial sidelines and engage in the battle to open up competition in higher education.

2. *Establish credential approval seals.* Limiting Washington's intervention in higher education and accreditation will provide opportunities for the business community to establish metrics, standards, and, ultimately, credentials for the coursework students take at various institutions, as well as other "real world" or internship experience. In order to provide independent assessments and credentials of course work and other skills, businesses, nonprofits, and other non-governmental entities should work to create "an educational analog of Underwriters Laboratories." By doing so, employers can help to assure future students that if they succeed in employer-credentialed courses, they will have a far greater chance of finding a job after graduation.

# Organizations to Contact

*The editors have compiled the following list of organizations concerned with the issues debated in this book. The descriptions are derived from materials provided by the organizations. All have publications or information available for interested readers. The list was compiled on the date of publication of the present volume; names, addresses, phone and fax numbers, and e-mail and Internet addresses may change. Be aware that many organizations take several weeks or longer to respond to inquiries, so allow as much time as possible.*

**American Association of Community Colleges (AACC)**
One Dupont Circle NW, Suite 410, Washington, DC 20036
(202) 728-0200 • fax: (202) 833-2467
website: www.aacc.nche.edu

The American Association of Community Colleges is the primary advocacy organization for the nation's community colleges. The association represents nearly twelve hundred two-year, associate degree-granting institutions and more than thirteen million students. AACC promotes community colleges through five strategic action areas: recognition and advocacy for community colleges; student access, learning, and success; community college leadership development; economic and workforce development; and global and intercultural education. Its publications include *Community College Journal* and *Community College Daily*.

**American Association of University Professors (AAUP)**
1133 Nineteenth St. NW, Suite 200, Washington, DC 20036
(202) 737-5900
e-mail: aaup@aaup.org
website: www.aaup.org

The mission of the American Association of University Professors is to advance academic freedom and shared governance; define fundamental professional values and standards for higher education; promote the economic security of faculty, academic professionals, graduate students, postdoctoral fellows, and all those engaged in teaching and research in higher education; help the higher education community organize to make our goals a reality; and ensure higher education's contribution to the common good. The association offers reports and publications on its website and publishes a monthly magazine, *Academe.*

## Brookings Institution

1775 Massachusetts Ave. NW, Washington, DC 20036-2188
(202) 797-6000
e-mail: communications@brookings.edu
website: www.brookings.edu

Founded in 1927, the Brookings Institution conducts research and publishes in the fields of government, foreign policy, economics, social sciences, and education. The institute publishes the *Brookings Review* quarterly as well as numerous books and research papers, including the Brookings Policy Brief Series. It has published a number of articles on numerous issues in higher education, many of which are available on its website.

## Campaign for America's Future

1825 K St. NW, Washington, DC 20006-1254
(202) 955-5665 • fax: (202) 955-5606
website: http://ourfuture.org

The Campaign for America's Future is a progressive research and advocacy organization whose goal is to forge the enduring progressive majority needed to achieve shared prosperity and equal opportunity in the United States. The organization advances a progressive economic agenda and a vision of the future that works for all, not simply the few, and addresses such issues as job security, income disparity, health care affordability, environment sustainability, and higher education. Its website includes a section titled Education Opportunity Network, which includes blogs, reports, and other resources dealing with the problems of higher education in the United States.

## Campaign for the Future of Higher Education (CFHE)
e-mail: info@futureofhighered.org
website: http://futureofhighered.org

The Campaign for the Future of Higher Education aims to guarantee that affordable, quality higher education is accessible to all sectors of our society in the coming decades and includes the voices of the faculty, staff, students, and communities in the process of making change. CFHE also works to ensure that the emphasis, curriculum, pricing, and structure of the nation's higher education systems are good for students and the quality of education they receive. Online, the organization provides numerous publications, including "Who Is Professor 'Staff'" and "How Can This Person Teach So Many Classes?"

## Heritage Foundation
214 Massachusetts Ave. NE, Washington, DC   20002-4999
(202) 546-4400
e-mail: info@heritage.org
website: www.heritage.org

The Heritage Foundation is a research and educational institution—a think tank—whose mission is to formulate and promote conservative public policies based on the principles of free enterprise, limited government, individual freedom, traditional American values, and a strong national defense. Its website offers news, articles, and in-depth publications on the costs of higher education, student loans, and the federal regulation of colleges and universities.

## National Center for Public Policy and Higher Education
5205 Prospect Rd., #135/279, San Jose, CA   95129
(408) 792-3140
e-mail: pcallan@highereducation.org
website: www.highereducation.org

The National Center for Public Policy and Higher Education promotes public policies that enhance Americans' opportunities to pursue education and training beyond high school. The center prepares action-oriented analyses of policy issues facing the states and the nation regarding opportunity and achievement in higher education. The center also communicates performance results and key findings to the public, civic, business, and higher education leaders along with state and federal officials.

## National Education Association (NEA)

1201 16th St. NW, Washington, DC   20036-3290
(202) 833-4000
website: www.nea.org

The National Education Association is a volunteer-based organization that represents 3.2 million public school teachers, university and college faculty members, college students training to be teachers, retired educators, and other educational professionals. Its mission is to advocate for educational professionals and support the goal of public education to prepare every student to succeed in a diverse world. It publishes books, newsletters, e-newsletters, and magazines, including its flagship publication, *NEAToday Magazine.*

## US Department of Education

400 Maryland Ave. SW, Washington, DC   20202
(800) 872-5327
website: www.ed.gov

Established in 1979, the US Department of Education aims to promote student achievement, establish policies on federal financial aid for education, focus national attention on key educational issues, and prohibit discrimination and ensure equal access to education. Its website offers sources for prospective and current college students, including information on student loans and college accreditation.

# Bibliography

## Books

Richard Arum and Josipa Roksa — *Academically Adrift: Limited Learning on College Campuses.* Chicago: University of Chicago Press, 2011.

Derek Bok — *Higher Education in America.* Princeton, NJ: Princeton University Press, 2013.

William G. Bowen — *Higher Education in the Digital Age.* Princeton, NJ: Princeton University Press, 2013.

Clayton M. Christensen and Henry J. Eyring — *The Innovative University: Changing the DNA of Higher Education from the Inside Out.* San Francisco: Jossey-Bass, 2011.

Allan Collins and Richard Halverson — *Rethinking Education in the Age of Technology: The Digital Revolution and Schooling in America.* New York: Teachers College Press, 2009.

Andrew Delbanco — *College: What It Was, Is, and Should Be.* Princeton, NJ: Princeton University Press, 2013.

Paul L. Gaston — *Higher Education Accreditation: How It's Changing, Why It Must.* Sterling, VA: Stylus Publishing, 2014.

Henry A. Giroux — *Neoliberalism's War on Higher Education.* Toronto, Canada: Between the Lines, 2014.

Andrew Hacker and Claudia Dreifus — *Higher Education?: How Colleges Are Wasting Our Money and Failing Our Kids—And What We Can Do About It.* New York: Times Books, 2010.

Suzanne Mettler — *Degrees of Inequality: How the Politics of Higher Education Sabotaged the American Dream.* New York: Basic Books, 2014.

Parker J. Palmer, Arthur Zajonc, and Megan Scribner — *The Heart of Higher Education: A Call to Renewal.* San Francisco: Jossey-Bass, 2010.

Jeffrey J. Selingo — *College (Un)bound: The Future of Higher Education and What It Means for Students.* Boston, MA: Houghton Mifflin Harcourt, 2013.

Jeffrey R. Young — *Beyond the MOOC Hype: A Guide to Higher Education's High-Tech Disruption.* Washington, DC: Chronicle of Higher Education, 2013.

## Periodicals and Internet Sources

ACT — "Changing Lives, Building a Workforce: Preparing Community College Students for Jobs and Careers," 2011. www.act.org.

Nanette Asimov — "Community College Dropout Rate Alarms Researchers," *San Francisco Chronicle*, October 20, 2010.

Allie Bidwell "Where Do MOOCs Fit in Higher Education?," *U.S. News & World Report*, May 15, 2014.

David D. Burnstein "Shai Reshef on Educating the World," *Fast Company*, December 8, 2011.

Nathan Heller "Laptop U," *New Yorker*, May 20, 2013.

Robert Hiltonsmith and Tamara Draut "The Great Cost Shift Continues: State Higher Education Funding After the Recession," Demos, March 6, 2014. www.demos.org.

Howard Hotson "Germany's Great Tuition Fees U-Turn," *Times Higher Education*, February 13, 2014. www .timeshighereducation.co.uk.

Doug Lederman "An Innovation Stifler?," *Inside Higher Ed*, February 17, 2014. www.insidehighered.com.

*Pittsburgh Quarterly* "A Crisis in Higher Education," Fall 2012.

Eduardo Porter "Dropping Out of College, and Paying the Price," *New York Times*, June 25, 2013.

Ginny Skalski "Internet Is Future of Higher Education Says University of the People," Opensource.com, August 27, 2013. http://opensource.com.

Catharine R. Stimpson

"On Becoming a Phoenix: Encounters with the Digital Revolution," *Chronicle of Higher Education*, October 1, 2012.

Das Williams

"Reinvest in Higher Education: California's Universities Need Funding Parity with Lower Schools," *Santa Barbara Independent*, May 14, 2014.

# Index

# M

# N

# O

# P

# Q

# R

# S

# T